# KNOW THE LANDSCAPE

# Estates and the English Countryside

# KNOW THE LANDSCAPE

# Estates and the English Countryside

## J. H. Bettey

'Wealth, Rank and Ostentation in the Landscape'

B.T. BATSFORD LTD · LONDON

© J.H. Bettey 1993

First published 1993

All rights reserved. No part of this publication may be
reproduced, in any form or by any means, without
permission from the Publisher

Typeset by Best-set Typesetter Ltd, Hong Kong
and printed in Great Britain by
The Bath Press, Avon

Published by B.T. Batsford Ltd
4 Fitzhardinge Street, London W1H 0AH

A CIP catalogue record for this book is
available from the British Library

ISBN 0 7134 6710 X

# Contents

# Illustrations

*Illustrations*

# Acknowledgements

I am indebted to numerous friends and colleagues for their helpful comments on earlier drafts of the following chapters and for their suggestions and help with illustrations. Any work of this sort must lean heavily on the detailed researches of many scholars, and the extent of my obligation is evident from the many publications cited in the notes. For detailed comment, criticisms and discussion I am particularly grateful to Michael Aston, James Bond, Michael Costen and Robert Machin; Dr Rodney Ambler, C.A. Buchanan, Dr David Hey and Dr Celia Miller provided illustrations and examples, as did N.A. Lee and M.T. Richardson of Bristol University Library Special Collections. The help of Gordon Kelsey and the Arts Faculty Photographic Unit of the University of Bristol was invaluable in the preparation of photographs. Much of the stimulus in pursuing the subject has come from the enthusiasm of the students who have studied this subject with me in courses arranged for the Department for Continuing Education of the University of Bristol.

# Note on county names

The problem of which county names to use to help the reader in locating the places mentioned in the book has been difficult. Apart from reluctance to use the post-1974 creations such as Avon or Humberside, which were devised with scant regard for historic traditions or local loyalties, and which are particularly inappropriate for a historical study, English local government is at the time of writing about to undergo yet another major reorganization.

It seems likely that this will alter even more of the ancient county boundaries and sweep away many of the county names including those of the new counties; it seemed best therefore to keep to the traditional pre-1974 county names throughout the book.

# Preface

The English countryside today bears witness to centuries of human activity and interference in numerous ways that can be interpreted by the informed observer using the skills of the archaeologist and the local historian. This new, wide-ranging series looks at the development of the landscape in Britain and examines the forces at work which have shaped its changing appearance from prehistoric times to the present day.

Each book takes a characteristic aspect of the landscape – such as the estates, monasteries, roads, canals and railways, traces its history and development, explains its function and studies its impact on the landscape throughout history. The subjects are popular and may have easily recognizable features that can still be visited and enjoyed, but some of the effects they have had on the landscape of today are subtle and unexpected and their influence has profoundly changed the look of the countryside around us.

For instance, castles and manor houses are still visible, but so too, to the trained eye, are their fishponds and kitchen gardens, long since demolished or destroyed above ground. What are the reasons behind barely discernible ditches and banks; why is an ancient track just where it is; why were certain villages deserted; less obviously, even why are some trees shaped the way they are? These are some of the intriguing questions discussed in this series.

The authors show how the techniques of landscape research can be used by anyone to enable them to recognize and decipher the signs of various periods of the human past in their own environment. They also guide the reader to some of the sources of documentary evidence and point out particular areas of research that can still be pursued, enabling the individual to make a real contribution.

The series builds up to present a new insight into familiar views and landscapes and brings out some of the hidden features of the British countryside.

# Introduction

For many centuries much of the English countryside has been dominated by estates – the lands of the Crown, the Duchy of Cornwall, the Duchy of Lancaster, the widespread landholdings of the Church and the domains of the aristocracy and gentry. The landscape has been moulded and structured under their influence.

In most parts of England the predominant influence of large landed estates upon the landscape is clearly recognizable. Not only is the elegant mansion, set within its landscaped park, enclosed within a massive wall and surrounded by carefully planted woodlands, distinctive lodges, well-built farms, estate cottages and landmarks, such a common feature of the English rural scene, but the impact of long ownership by a single wealthy family or institution can be observed in a host of other features. The village houses are frequently built in one style and commonly bear a coat of arms, initials or other distinguishing feature, the village school is often the gift of the landlord, as are the almshouses, parish hall and church rooms, while the inn bears the family name and arms. The church generally has been drastically restored or even rebuilt at the landlord's expense, and the family pew, ornate monuments, hatchments and burial vault are often a prominent, and occasionally an overwhelming, aspect of the interior. Neatly enclosed fields, wide roads, uniform woodlands, game coverts and landscape features such as obelisks, towers or other 'eye-catchers' are also hallmarks of ownership by a great estate.

From the time of the Roman occupation, and in many regions for long before, much of the English countryside has been dominated by great estates and major landholdings, and it is this concentration of ownership over the centuries which has had such a profound effect upon the appearance of the landscape. Some estate boundaries have been remarkably persistent features of the landscape, and recent work in many parts of the country has demonstrated the way in which some modern parishes and other administrative divisions preserve the boundaries of Anglo-Saxon estates or possibly even of Roman land-units.[1]

The word 'estate' needs some explanation since it can be used in various different ways, and over the centuries major landholdings have assumed many forms. Not all of these have been cohesive units, their size and character have been infinitely varied, and many have formed part of scattered royal, ecclesiastical or baronial possessions. Here the term estate is taken to mean any landholding of at least 3000 acres, subject to a single owner, whether an institution or an individual, not necessarily made up of a single compact territory, but which has been administered as a unit and where the effects of a single ownership can be recognized.

Estates have included the territories of local leaders during the Iron Age, the lands of Roman villas, Saxon lordships and complex estates, royal castles, palaces and forests, the properties of bishops and religious houses, the lands of medieval lords and the domains of the aristocracy and gentry. All these owners have in their different ways imposed their ideas, purposes and character upon the landscape of their estates and upon the buildings, farms, woodlands, parks and gardens which they created. For a fuller discussion of the development of parks and gardens the reader is referred to another volume in this series: Anthea Taigel and Tom Williamson *Parks and Gardens* (1993). The purpose of this book is to show the effect the different kinds of estate have had upon the landscape since the Norman Conquest, and to examine their legacy to the modern countryside. It also shows the way the landscape has been changed as each generation of owners, with total confidence in their own taste, swept away the work of their predecessors and used their wealth to create the contemporary concept of an ideal environment – to impress their neighbours or to advertise their social status and political importance.

Not all parts of the country have been similarly affected by estate owners, and many areas did not form part of the territory of a single major landowner, but over large stretches of England, from populous Midland villages to remote and hilly moorland, the influence of estate ownership was paramount. Precise figures of land ownership are not available until the later nineteenth century, when in 1872–3 detailed statistics were collected and published by order of Parliament in 1874 as *Return of Owners of Land*.[2] This Return provides for the first time accurate details concerning the possessions of landowners, the extent of their income from land and the size of their estates. It also reveals the vast possessions and enormous incomes enjoyed by some individual landowners. Obviously the value of estates varied greatly, depending, for

## GREAT ESTATES

*Counties in order of the proportion of total area (excluding waste) occupied by estates which in aggregate exceeded 10,000 acres.*

| Percentage of total area | | | |
|---|---|---|---|
| 1. Rutland | 53 | 21. Hampshire | 21 |
| 2. Northumberland | 50 | 22. Shropshire | 21 |
| 3. Nottingham | 38 | 23. Devon | 20 |
| 4. Dorset | 36 | 24. Somerset | 20 |
| 5. Wiltshire | 36 | 25. Buckingham | 19 |
| 6. Cheshire | 35 | 26. Cumberland | 19 |
| 7. Derby | 31 | 27. Leicester | 19 |
| 8. Stafford | 31 | 28. Norfolk | 19 |
| 9. Northampton | 30 | 29. Berkshire | 17 |
| 10. Yorkshire | 28 | 30. Huntingdon | 17 |
| 11. Durham | 28 | 31. Gloucester | 16 |
| 12. Lincoln | 28 | 32. Worcester | 16 |
| 13. Westmorland | 27 | 33. Oxford | 15 |
| 14. Cornwall | 27 | 34. Kent | 12 |
| 15. Bedford | 24 | 35. Cambridge | 11 |
| 16. Lancashire | 24 | 36. Hereford | 11 |
| 17. Warwick | 24 | 37. Surrey | 10 |
| 18. Hertford | 23 | 38. Essex | 9 |
| 19. Sussex | 23 | 39. Middlesex | 4 |
| 20. Suffolk | 22 | | |

*Average for all England*: 24 per cent

instance, on the quality of the soil, the proximity of towns and markets, the presence of coal, minerals and quarries or of industrial potential, but if a *great estate* is defined as comprising more than 10,000 acres and a *large estate* as possessing a minimum of 3000 acres, then the Return of 1874 showed that 24 per cent of England was occupied by *great estates* and 17 per cent by *large estates*. There were wide regional differences, and the north and west of England had a much higher proportion of estates than the south or east, while the demand for land in the counties around London prevented the creation of many major estates there. For example, among Wiltshire landowners, the Marquess of Bath, whose seat was at Longleat, owned 55,000 acres, the Earl of Pembroke who

## LARGE ESTATES

*Counties in order of total area (excluding waste) occupied by estates of 3000 to 10,000 acres.*

| | Percentage of total area | | | |
|---|---|---|---|---|
| 1. Shropshire | 31 | 21. Yorkshire | 18 |
| 2. Huntingdon | 27 | 22. Northampton | 17 |
| 3. Hereford | 25 | 23. Devon | 17 |
| 4. Oxford | 25 | 24. Hertford | 17 |
| 5. Hampshire | 24 | 25. Nottingham | 17 |
| 6. Berkshire | 22 | 26. Stafford | 17 |
| 7. Norfolk | 22 | 27. Suffolk | 17 |
| 8. Buckingham | 21 | 28. Cheshire | 16 |
| 9. Gloucester | 21 | 29. Cornwall | 16 |
| 10. Kent | 21 | 30. Derby | 16 |
| 11. Northumberland | 21 | 31. Surrey | 16 |
| 12. Worcester | 20 | 32. Bedford | 15 |
| 13. Essex | 19 | 33. Durham | 13 |
| 14. Sussex | 19 | 34. Lincoln | 13 |
| 15. Leicester | 18 | 35. Cambridge | 12 |
| 16. Warwick | 18 | 36. Lancashire | 12 |
| 17. Dorset | 18 | 37. Middlesex | 11 |
| 18. Rutland | 18 | 38. Westmorland | 11 |
| 19. Somerset | 18 | 39. Cumberland | 10 |
| 20. Wiltshire | 18 | | |

*Average for all England: 17 per cent*[3]

lived at Wilton owned 42,000 acres, and the Marquess of Ailesbury had an estate centred on Tottenham House in Savernake Forest comprising 55,000 acres, of which 38,000 lay within Wiltshire.

In Bedfordshire the Duke of Bedford possessed 33,500 acres with an estimated gross rental of £47,500, apart from his lands elsewhere and his highly lucrative London properties. The Duke of Northumberland's estate centred on Alnwick Castle comprised 181,600 acres giving an annual income of £162,000; the Earl of Orford commanded over 12,000 acres in Norfolk; the Duke of Westminster's lands in Cheshire amounted to 15,000 acres with an annual rental of £32,000, and an even larger sum came from his extremely valuable estate in London. The Duke of Marlborough owned 22,000 acres in Oxfordshire worth £34,000 per annum. The Earl of Derby possessed 57,000 acres in Lancashire, much of it highly profitable mining and industrial land which brought the staggeringly large annual income of £157,000; while the Duke of Sutherland's estate of 30,000 acres in Shropshire and Staffordshire was dwarfed in size, though not in value, by more than a million acres of Scottish moorland which he possessed in Sutherland. The Earl of Harewood owned 29,000 acres of the West Riding of Yorkshire worth £37,000 per annum; and the Earl of Carlisle had 13,000 acres centred upon his mansion at Castle Howard (Yorkshire), and a further 65,000 acres in Cumberland and Northumberland. The full figures for major landholding in each English county are as shown in the two tables.

It was these large landholdings and the vast wealth they provided which enabled many of their owners to dominate the social and political scene, and to have such a profound effect on the landscape, creating the mansions, farmsteads, parks, gardens, churches, lodges and model villages which form the subject of this book. Until the seventeenth century the value of a landed estate to its owner was much more than the income which it represented or the worth of the lands, farms and cottages of which it was comprised. An estate provided a residence and a setting commensurate with the owner's wealth and social status – the ownership of widespread lands brought with it political power and local patronage. Above all, it provided a visible and public statement of position within the community, and the possibility for an ostentatious display of fortune, authority and influence. The possession of an estate and a country seat was the essential qualification for membership of the ruling elite in each county, or for social and political progress in the wider spheres of London and in particular Westminster.

# 1 Medieval estates: conquest and military power

Throughout the Middle Ages, and for long afterwards, land was the crucial feature of all relationships, military, financial, tenurial, political and personal, upon which society was based. Society continued to be rooted in the soil and rich and poor alike were equally dependent on the profits and produce of agricultural estates and at the mercy of all the perils to which farming enterprises are subject.

For the English landscape, as for so many other aspects of English life, major changes took place in the decades following the Norman Conquest in 1066. Some earlier estates continued with only minor changes, but in most places the Saxon landowners were replaced by a much smaller number of energetic Norman lords chosen from the military adventurers who had followed William on his risky enterprise, who owed their position to the King and who derived their title from military conquest. Likewise, Normans took over the key positions in Church and State. The new lords were quick to impose tighter and harsher conditions of feudal service upon their tenants, and many also emphasized their dependence on military conquest by erecting castles on their estates. A further long-term consequence of the Norman Conquest was that the sixty Benedictine monasteries which between them possessed about 15 per cent of the land of England in 1066, were increased by many new foundations, especially by endowments given to the newer orders – the Cluniacs,

Cistercians, Carthusians, Augustinians and Premonstratensians – in the wave of religious enthusiasm that swept through England during the twelfth century. The same period also saw a great proliferation of churches and chapelries as manorial lords founded or rebuilt places of worship on their estates; in many parts of England this led to the curious feature of two parish churches being found very close together. At Willingale Doe and Willingale Spain (Essex) two parish churches are in one churchyard, as are the two churches at South Walsham (Norfolk) or Swaffham Prior (Cambridgeshire). Elsewhere there are many examples of churches founded on manorial boundaries which are in close proximity, as at Alvingham and North Cockerington (Lincolnshire), Eastleach Turville and Eastleach Martin (Gloucestershire) or Alton Barnes and Alton Priors (Wiltshire). The building of new churches and energetic reconstruction of old ones provides impressive evidence of the proprietorial attitude which the Norman overlords adopted towards their churches, as well as of their piety and practical concern for the religious life of their tenants.

The Norman castles were intended to dominate their surroundings and were a constant, visible reminder to the populace that they were under the control of new and powerful overlords. The castles provided a residence and an administrative centre for each estate, a base for military operations

**1**   *Motte and bailey, at Nether Stowey (Somerset). An example of the fortifications which were erected by the Norman conquerors to overawe the countryside and proclaim the arrival of a new ruling class.*

and an impressive symbol of power in the landscape. They varied in size, with the great majority consisting of a motte, or mound, with a wooden tower, or keep, on the top, and possibly also a defensive palisade or wall around the bailey. Much less numerous were the stone-built castles, erected by the Crown or by greater nobles, and intended to emphasize authority and to overawe a whole region. Hundreds of simple fortifications, defensive works or motte and bailey castles were built all over the country in the decades following the Conquest (Fig. 1), and those hastily constructed by William himself at Pevensey,

Hastings and Dover are depicted on the Bayeux Tapestry. This shows in remarkable detail men engaged in throwing up earth to create the mound on which the castle at Hastings was to be built. Many of the wooden castles were short-lived affairs, and numerous similar structures were erected during the harsh conditions of the Civil War between King Stephen and the Empress Matilda during the first half of the twelfth century.

These artificial castle mounds survive as impressive archaeological features in many parts of the country. On the flat clays of Bedfordshire the great mounds of the former castles at Yielden and Cainhoe are spectacular features of the landscape. Some were eventually replaced by stone castles, such as the castle built at Dover which continued to have an important military and strategic function until the Second World War, or the string of massively fortified and grimly impressive castles built along the Welsh border. Great royal castles occupied strategic sites such as Richmond (Yorkshire), Bamburgh (Northumberland), Corfe Castle (Dorset) or the Peak (Derbyshire), others dominated important towns like London, Canterbury, Bristol, Winchester, York, Norwich, Lincoln, Nottingham or Warwick. The surviving Norman castles and the earthworks of former castles provide an enduring and impressive symbol of the power of the new conquerors of England, and the forcible employment of great numbers of English labourers upon their construction must have given many their first intimate and unhappy acquaintance with their new rulers.[1]

## The Domesday Survey

Some indication of the estates of the new Norman overlords emerges from the detailed technical descriptions contained in the Domesday Survey of 1086. Compared to later estates, a striking feature is the dispersed nature of many of the holdings, which was possibly a deliberate policy of the Conqueror to check the potential for rebellion among his most powerful adherents by preventing them from building up a strong power-base in any one area of the country. An exception was in the unruly north and along the vulnerable Welsh border, where the Conqueror created large lordships or 'honours' such as those of Chester, Shrewsbury, Lancaster, Pontefract, Wakefield and Richmond, each with its major castle intended to establish Norman control.

The great barony granted to one of William's principal followers, William de Warenne, consisted of large blocks of land in Sussex and Norfolk, with smaller estates scattered through Hampshire, Cambridgeshire, Suffolk, Oxfordshire, Buckinghamshire, West Yorkshire and several other counties. The greater part of this huge estate was leased out to knights, and the majority of landlords with whom the tenants in Norman England came into contact were the occupants of these much smaller properties rather than the great barons. The Survey shows that the Normans had acquired a settled land with ancient administrative and ecclesiastical boundaries, and where most of the good agricultural land was already being exploited. Sheep were by far the most numerous animals, and there are also occasional references to specialized dairy farms (*vaccaria*) and to cheese-making, for example in the Thames valley and the Vale of the White Horse. Managed woodland, mills, salt works and fisheries were to be found in various parts of the country, and in addition to large amounts of fish, the fisheries along the major rivers such as the Severn, Ouse, Thames and Trent and in the Fens and the Somerset Levels also produced enormous quantities of eels.

The Survey also provides evidence that within two decades of the Conquest the Normans were encouraging the spread of a new element on their estates. At 55 places in the south and east of England, from Somerset to the Isle of Ely, vineyards are listed, and although there were a few vineyards in Anglo-Saxon England, it seems likely that the Normans had greatly increased the number. The largest vineyard was at Bisham (Berkshire) which was said to be some 12 acres or more in extent. There were four vineyards in Wiltshire, and at one of them, Wilcot in the Vale of Pewsey, even the usually dry and formal words of the Domesday surveyor managed to show the small estate there as prosperous and attractive, for it was said to have *ecclesia nova, domus optima et vinea bona* (a new church, an excellent house and a good vineyard).[2]

## Forests

The best-known and most long-lasting effect of the Norman Conquest was the creation of the royal forests and the many hunting grounds or chases, as well as parks and warrens throughout England. The Normans also imposed the Forest Law, a major legal innovation with mercilessly severe penalties, upon whole regions of the country. The *Anglo-Saxon Chronicle* saw this as the most wicked of the Norman misdeeds, and complained of William that

> He set apart a vast deer preserve and imposed
> Laws concerning it.
> Whoever slew a hart or a hind
> Was to be blinded.
> He forbade the killing of boars
> Even as the killing of harts.
> For he loved the tall stags dearly
> As though he had been their father.

Later chroniclers, no doubt with considerable exaggeration, lamented the villages laid waste and the sorrowful people driven from their homes. Kings and noblemen had loved hunting long before the Norman Conquest. King Edmund had narrowly escaped death while hunting at Cheddar (Somerset) in 943, and the laws of Cnut had laid heavy penalties on those who hunted the king's deer; but it was the Norman kings who introduced the Forest Laws and who created huge areas of royal forest. Such areas were not necessarily wooded, and the word 'forest' was a legal concept applied to lands set apart with their own special laws, outside the common law of England. The creation of the royal forests was a gradual process, and by the time of the Domesday Survey of 1086 no more than 25 were in existence, whereas during the next

century the number was increased more than threefold until the forests covered a third of the country. Two of the largest, created by the Conqueror himself, were the great forest of Windsor, which eventually extended over much of eastern Berkshire as well as covering parts of Buckinghamshire, Surrey and Middlesex, and the huge area of the New Forest in Hampshire which occupied some 100,000 acres.

The creation of the New Forest was greatly resented by those who found themselves living within its boundaries, and many of the myths which were fostered about the destruction and evictions involved have survived through the centuries. There is no doubt that the setting aside of such a large expanse was a vast undertaking, and that it reflects the power, arrogance and high-handed methods of the Norman conquerors. But the soil of the area is mostly poor sands and gravel which did not support a large population, and the view that a flourishing and prosperous district had been laid to waste in order to provide a hunting ground, and that the inhabitants had ruthlessly been driven out, is a great exaggeration. The Domesday Survey devotes a separate section to the New Forest, and shows that a number of settlements remained within its bounds and there is little evidence of wholesale eviction or destruction, although just over the Wiltshire border at Downton there was some land from which 'the inhabitants have fled because of the King's forest'. There can be no doubt of the unpopularity of the forest and the forest laws. When William Rufus was killed while hunting in the New Forest in 1100 contemporaries were quick to ascribe his death to the hand of God raised in retribution for the hardship caused to the people of the forest. The chronicler Florence of Worcester wrote that

Doubtless, as common report has it, this was verily the righteous vengeance of God. For in days of old, that is in the days of King Edward and other Kings of England before him, that land flourished plentifully with country-folk, with worshippers of God and with churches; but at the bidding of King William the Elder, men were driven away, their houses thrown down, their churches destroyed, and the land kept as an abiding-place for beasts of the chase; and thence it is believed was the cause of the mischance.

Many other royal forests covered vast areas, such as Dartmoor, Essex, Pickering, Sherwood, High Peak and the Forest of Dean, and although the amount of land designated as forest declined considerably during the later Middle Ages, remnants survived in many parts of England until the major disafforestation during the reign of Charles I and the upheavals of the Civil War brought about the destruction of all but a few.

Within the forest areas the beasts of the chase were the red and roe deer and, from the twelfth century, the fallow deer which, like the rabbit, was imported by the Normans and soon became common in England. During the early Middle Ages the wild boar was also to be found in the forests, as well as the wolf. As late as 1210 King John gave 15 shillings to two huntsmen who killed two wolves at Gillingham (Dorset) and another at Clarendon near Salisbury, although the fact that he gave so much may suggest that the creatures were rare by that time. There are occasional references to wolves in the later thirteenth century, and, for example, in 1295 the king's huntsman was paid 11s 8d for catching wolves in Middleton Stoney Park (Oxfordshire).

The forests prevented or greatly hindered any extension of cultivated land or any agricultural improvement. Clearly not even the most dedicated royal lover of hunting could follow the sport in every royal forest, even if he neglected all other duties, and most of the royal forests therefore came to be used to provide the luxury of fresh

venison for the royal palaces for feasts, or were a source of timber for royal use or as gifts, and of underwood, fuel and minerals for sale. For example, the forest of Pamber on the northern boundary of Hampshire provided regular supplies of oak trees during the thirteenth and fourteenth centuries. Many were used for the building of royal palaces, castles and residences in London and at Kingsclere (Hampshire), Winchester Castle and Old Sarum; others were sent as gifts from the Crown to Westminster Abbey and other religious houses in London, Reading, Oxford, Winchester and elsewhere. Some deer from the forest were also supplied to the royal household but the quantity was never very large because of the depredations of poachers.[3]

Throughout the Middle Ages 'assarts' or piecemeal enclosures were made in many royal forests as farmers gradually nibbled at the edges or extended their cultivated land. Fines imposed upon those who had brought forest land into cultivation formed a useful source of royal revenue. Thus at Whiteparish (Wiltshire) within the royal forest of Melchet, 14 tenants were fined for making assarts in 1270, and in 1330 fines were imposed for the assarting of a further 73 acres. The small, irregular fields which resulted from this process, with their substantial banks or hedges, are still evident in the landscape of Whiteparish and are a reminder of the way in which these fields were laboriously hacked out of thick woodland and slowly cleared of tree stumps, stones and other obstacles to the plough.[4] All classes of medieval society were engaged in this slow process of assarting, and, for example, at the end of the twelfth century Richard I pardoned the canons of Waltham Abbey for intakes from the forests on their estates in Essex and Berkshire totalling more than 405ha (1000 acres), while under King John the Cistercians of Stanley abbey (Wiltshire) were fined the huge sum of £667 for similar enclosures. At the other end of the social scale, the manorial court rolls of Gillingham (Dorset) for 1302 record that 'Walter atte Wodeseyned gives to the Lady Queen twelve pence for a perch and a half encroachment opposite his gate, paying for rent due a penny a year'.[5]

Parts of former royal forests have survived through the centuries and are still clearly recognizable, such as Savernake Forest (Wiltshire), Sherwood Forest (Nottinghamshire), the Forest of Dean (Gloucestershire) or the New Forest (Hampshire). Some also retain the remains of royal hunting lodges or residences, such as King's Court in the former forest of Gillingham (Dorset), Bagden Lodge in Savernake Forest, the manor house and later royal residence at Woodstock within Wychwood Forest, or the greatest of all the royal retreats and hunting palaces, Clarendon near Salisbury, built by Henry II and greatly enlarged and sumptuously furnished by Henry III. Clarendon was not fortified, but was an opulent palace, intended for comfortable living, with a great hall, apartments, chapels, kitchens, stables and other buildings covering an area of about 2.5ha (6 acres). The palace continued to be used by English monarchs throughout the Middle Ages, but with the disafforestation of the royal forest it was abandoned and fell into ruin, so that today only a fragment of walling remains of what was one of the most splendid of medieval royal residences, and the site is overwhelmed by numerous trees and by undergrowth.

Other forests are recognizable from place-names such as those relating to deer, hounds or hunting or to the management of the forest. For example, within the forests, enclosures for deer were maintained which were known as 'hays' and the former forest of Cannock retains numerous names such as Alrewas Hay, Teddesley Hay, Gailey Hay, Cheslyn Hay and several other similar ones can be found.

## Chases and parks

In addition to the royal forests, individual lords or great ecclesiastics also acquired from the Crown rights to hunt over certain specified areas known as 'chases'. Thus the Earl of Warwick was granted an area of 2500 acres at Sutton Coldfield (Warwickshire) by Henry I, out of the large area of Cannock Forest, to make a great chase or hunting ground, a sizeable part of which survives as Sutton Park. The Earls of Dudley had chases at Pensnett and Baggeridge (Staffordshire), while the Bishop of Coventry and Lichfield was granted part of the forest of Cannock to create Cannock Chase by Richard I in return for donations to a crusade. Cranborne Chase (Dorset) was granted to the Earls of Gloucester by William Rufus but later reverted to the Crown; King John frequently hunted there and possessed a royal house or hunting lodge at Tollard Royal (Wiltshire). During the Middle Ages there were more than 30 large chases in various parts of England, and within them the owners exercised as tight a control on hunting and other rights as did the Crown officials within the royal forests.[6]

Smaller but much more numerous are the medieval deer parks, many of which have left a considerable imprint upon the landscape. Deer kept within a park were securely enclosed since they are such agile creatures, able to jump surprisingly high fences. The boundaries, which generally consisted of an earthen bank topped by a fence of cleft oak stakes or by a stone wall, had to be formidable, and sometimes also incorporated a 'deer-leap' which enabled the deer to jump into the park but not to get out again. Deer parks varied greatly in size from a few acres to several hundred, and their purpose was to confine the deer so that they would be available for hunting or could easily be killed for food. The park surrounding the royal palace at Clarendon was more than 5km (3 miles) in diameter, while the bank along the south side of John of Gaunt's deer park at King's Somborne (Hampshire) is still 3.6m (12ft) high. In Yorkshire, Sheffield Park comprised 2461 acres (1000ha), while in the East Riding alone there were more than 30 deer parks. Tankersley Park in the West Riding was created in the early fourteenth century and its boundaries can still be followed along 7km (4½ miles) of footpaths, hedges and walls. An engraving of *c.*1725 shows the park still completely surrounded by a prodigious stone wall.[7] The Earl of Arundel possessed 12 parks in Sussex and several others in Surrey, while the Archbishop of Canterbury enjoyed the facilities of 18 parks on his estates in Kent and Sussex.

The county of Staffordshire contained more than 100 parks, some of them very large like Lord Stafford's great park at Madeley, and others more modest like the 160 acres which the Dean of Wolverhampton was licensed to enclose with a bank and ditch at Blakesley to reserve it as a deer park. Park banks were very substantial earthworks and many remain as obvious features of the modern landscape. Harbin's Park in the parish of Tarrant Gunville near Blandford Forum on the Dorset chalkland covers 47ha (115 acres) and is still completely enclosed by a massive bank with an internal ditch which would have effectively deprived the deer of any possibility of jumping over the park pales.

Cattle were also kept within the confines of parks, and Chartley Park (Staffordshire) which contained a distinctive strain of medieval cattle, was created out of the forest of Needwood in *c.*1279.[8] Likewise, the distinctive medieval breed of white cattle survives at Chillingham Park in Northumberland. The small county of Hertfordshire contained no less than 40 parks by the end of the Middle Ages. A new park made at Kings Langley in 1290 was described as containing 8 acres of former meadow land and 120 acres of land which

had been arable. The park, banks and fences needed constant repair and attention if the deer were not to escape, and work on the park fences was an onerous burden imposed on many tenants by landlords. The Bishop of Chichester required his tenants for many miles around to work annually on the fences around his park at Aldingbourne, and to assist with the hunting for several days each year; and a thirteenth-century custumal (a statement of the ancient customs and the obligations of tenants) of Glastonbury Abbey lists three days work each year on the park fences around the abbot's park at Pilton as one of the obligations of its tenants there and of tenants on nearby manors belonging to the abbey.

At Writtle (Essex) the park within the royal forest was described in a survey of 1328 as having a circuit of 2½ leagues; and one of the obligations of the tenants living on the royal manor was to maintain ten perches of the park pale. They were to be provided with the necessary timber which was to be split into pieces of a size that a man might carry, and they were allowed to keep any old or defective pales which they replaced. The bishops of Bath and Wells had numerous deer parks on their estates, and the bank around the park at Banwell was evidently topped with stakes, for during the reign of Henry VII certain poachers were accused of killing the bishop's deer at night and of setting their heads on the park pales in defiance of the bishop. Churchmen had the advantage that they could use the canon law of the Church as well as the civil law against poachers, and in 1341 the bishop of Worcester excommunicated those who had broken into his park at Henbury in Saltmarsh (Gloucestershire), hunted his deer and discharged arrows at them. Later this sentence was commuted to the confiscation of the poachers' weapons and they were obliged to offer candles at one of the bishop's churches.[9]

Deer parks could also be used for other

purposes – they could include fishponds and rabbit warrens (see below); the sale of timber and underwood could provide some profit; cattle could be grazed in them during the summer months; and some were also used for horse breeding. The Crown and the abbots of Welbeck and Basingstoke had large stud farms in their parks within the forest of High Peak during the fourteenth century, and Thomas of Lancaster had a stud with more than 100 mares in his park at High Duffield (Derbyshire) in 1322. In his park at Macclesfield in the fourteenth century, the Black Prince had a famous stud for breeding war-horses.[10]

The survival of so many impressive remnants of the huge enclosures which surrounded former deer parks, together with the numerous ancient 'park' and 'lodge' names, provides a reminder of how common deer parks once were as a profitable adjunct to many estates and as a notable feature of the landscape. Although they did provide a convenient source of venison and could also be used for some other purposes, deer parks were chiefly prized for the status they provided, since the costs of maintenance, feed for the deer, the wages of keepers and protection from poachers, meant that they were an expensive luxury and an example of conspicuous expenditure by estate owners.

The making of deer parks continued throughout the Middle Ages as is shown by part of the inscription on the large monument in Ashbourne church (Derbyshire) erected in 1537 to Sir Thomas Cockayne:

Three goodly houses he did build to his great
    praise and fame,
With profits great and manifold belonging to the
    same.
Three parks he did impale, therein to chase the
    deer
The lofty lodge within the park he also builded
    here.

## Fishponds and moats

Forests, chases and parks not only gave evidence of the status of those privileged to have rights within them, but could also be used to produce food. The park pales or fences provided protection for fishponds, rabbit warrens, hare enclosures and dovecots.

Fish was an extremely important item of medieval diet and sea fish were widely available throughout the country even in inland towns. The cellarer's account of Durham priory during the fifteenth century contains references to no less than 65 different kinds of fish and shell-fish used for food in the priory, and the late-medieval cellarer's account book of Tavistock Abbey shows frequent purchases of cod, hake, bass, ling, herring, mackerel and pilchards as well as the provision of great quantities of salmon which were caught in the Tamar.[11] Bicester priory in Oxfordshire also purchased large quantities of sea fish each year from the late thirteenth century, and in 1302, for example, no less than 10,000 herrings were bought for the priory kitchen. The two chaplains of Munden's chantry at Bridport during the fifteenth century consumed large amounts of salted cod, ling, hake and whiting, and for their Lenten diet also bought haddock, conger eel and herring, as well as oysters.[12]

For the wealthy members of society, however, the consumption of dried or salted sea fish was supplemented by the highly-prized and correspondingly expensive fresh fish, which were carefully bred and nurtured in fishponds. Every county in England, including coastal counties where fresh sea fish were readily available, had numerous fishponds, ranging from simple pools to vast and complex arrangements of waterworks providing breeding tanks, and separate ponds for rearing, fattening and storage. Like deer parks, fishponds were expensive to build and maintain and were essentially an adjunct of wealthy, aristocratic households and estates, or part of the possessions of well-endowed monasteries, and the many surviving remains are normally found in the parks or purlieus of castles, moated sites or religious houses. The number of former ponds which are recognizable in the landscape, and the numerous documentary references in medieval estate accounts or monastic expenses, bear witness to great efficiency in providing this sought-after component of medieval diet.

Many fishponds were on royal estates, like the royal manor of Feckenham (Worcestershire) where a new and expensive fishpond was built in 1169. In 1204 its repair and enlargement cost the huge sum of £40, and thereafter there are frequent references in the royal accounts to expenditure on the pond, and to gifts of bream from it. At Somerham (Huntingdonshire) the medieval bishops of Ely had a palace which included two very large fishponds; there was also a moat with a stone bridge and to the south a huge deer park which was said to be ten miles in circuit by the sixteenth century.[13] In Yorkshire the Sutton family paid an annual rent of 4000 eels to the Norman Count of Aumale for the lands they held at Sutton on Hull, and Domesday Book records that an annual render of 7000 eels was paid from the fishery at Beverley.

Moats could also be used as fishponds, for example in 1171 the bishop of Lincoln established a fishpond in the moat surrounding his manor house at Stow (Lincolnshire). William More, the prior of Worcester from 1518 until the dissolution in 1536, had several fishponds on his granges at Battenhall, Grimley and Hallow, and he built or enlarged a moat around his manor house at Crowle in 1533 at a total cost of £8 19s 3d and stocked the moat with fish. Prior More's ponds at Battenhall and his moat at Crowle are still clearly visible. Supplies of fish to stock his ponds were purchased from

fishermen along the nearby Severn, and in his journal More refers to eels, tench, bream, perch, roach and 'pickerels' or small pike. Even after the suppression of his house in 1536 More continued to enjoy regular meals of fresh fish, since he retired to Crowle where he had thoroughly renovated the manor house in the years before the dissolution, and lived there until his death in 1558. The expense of maintaining fishponds and the importance which More obviously attached to them can be seen from the fact that in 16 years he spent £47 15s 3d on his ponds plus the wages, food and drink for his own labourers, at a time when the weekly expenses of his large household amounted to no more than £1 0s 0d.[14]

The remains of a remarkable series of fishponds survive at Harrington (Northamptonshire) on an estate which belonged to the Knights Hospitallers from 1288 until the sixteenth century. They were situated in a steep-sided valley, and the remains of three large ponds, each with its own massive dam, and an elaborate system of water channels make this one of the best examples of medieval fishpond construction in the country. 'The whole system of the supply and overflow channels is a remarkable example of medieval engineering.'[15] Another fine complex of medieval fishponds in Northamptonshire survives at Silverstone on a former royal estate within the forest of Whittlewood. Again, there is a large dam to retain the water and a series of channels feeding the former breeding tanks and large pool. Royal records also show regular expenditure on the maintenance and stocking of fishponds as well as orders for the supply of fish to royal palaces at Woodstock and London.[16]

Because freshwater fish was so highly prized and so expensive, fishponds had constantly to be guarded from poachers, and medieval estate records contain many instances of fish being stolen. Again the ecclesiastical landlords had an advantage over laymen in that they could impose penalties which were valid in both this world and the next. Thus in 1329 Adam de Orleton, bishop of Worcester, excommunicated those who stole fish from the rector of Wellington.

... certain sons of iniquity whose names are unknown, casting aside the fear of God and paying no heed to such sentence, entered the close of Dom John de Clive, rector of Wellington, against the will of the appointed guardian, took fish from the stewpond there and carried them off to the peril of their souls, the prejudice of ecclesiastical liberty, the pernicious example of the people and the not inconsiderable loss of the rector.[17]

One of the most impressive fisheries to survive in the landscape is Meare Pool in Somerset which belonged to Glastonbury Abbey and which, throughout the Middle Ages, provided a regular supply of fish and eels for the numerous occupants of this great religious house. At the time of the suppression of the monastery the pool was described as

a great mere, which is 5 miles compass, being a mile and a half distant from the house, well replenished with great pike, bream, perch and roach.

By the side of the monastic pool at Meare and close to one of the monastic manor houses, a substantial fish house was built in the fourteenth century, and this survives although the pool has long since been drained (Fig. 2). The two-storey fish house provided accommodation for the fisherman and a place in which to dry and salt the fish and store boats and nets. Its fine

**2**  *Fish house at Meare (Somerset). This fourteenth-century fish house belonged to Glastonbury Abbey and stood beside the large lake or mere. It served as a lodging for the fisherman and a store house for his tackle, and is an example of the intensive way in which monasteries exploited all the resources of their estates.*

construction is a reminder of the value of the fishery to the abbey and of the way in which the monasteries exploited all the resources of their estates. There is evidence that the Glastonbury Abbey pool at Meare was also used for fishing as a recreation or sport, since a Survey of the abbey properties made at the time of the Dissolution early in 1540 lists the manor house at Meare with its garden and orchard, and also 'a pretty house for the fishers to drink in adjoining the same house . . . [and] . . . an old thatched house to store their fishing boats'. The survey goes on to mention the attractive views over the lake, the excellence of the fishing and the many swans, herons and pheasants to be found there.[18]

## Rabbits and pigeons

Rabbit warrens might also be found within the confines of parks. Rabbits or coneys were introduced into England from the Mediterranean region after the Norman Conquest, and throughout the Middle Ages their meat was regarded as a great delicacy; they were kept to supply the tables of the rich and were remarkably expensive. Their fur was also a valuable commodity. Unlike their modern successors which became such a ubiquitous pest and destroyers of crops, medieval rabbits were delicate creatures, requiring careful treatment if they were to survive the English climate or the perils of foxes, stoats and weasels. Specially constructed burrows were provided for them and their various warrens were fenced to keep out predators and poachers, and hay and other food were provided during the winter.

Reminders of such enclosures survive in place-names such as conygre or warren, and the evidence of the artificial burrows remains as 'pillow-mounds' – low elongated heaps of earth in which the burrows for the rabbits were constructed. Examples may be seen in the Warren at Hatfield Forest (Essex), in Ashdown Forest (Sussex), in Dolebury Warren within the Iron Age hillfort south of Bristol, on Minchinhampton Common near Stroud (Gloucestershire) or at several places on Dartmoor and Exmoor, including Warren Farm on Exmoor and at Ditsworthy (Devon).[19] Much of the poorer land on the Yorkshire Wolds and the East Anglian Brecklands during the later Middle Ages was given over to rabbit warrens and there were numerous warrens on the Isles of Scilly. Leases of abbey lands on the Isle of Wight during the fifteenth century include regular references to rabbit warrens and a recent historian of Quarr abbey has stated that

the very frequent documentary references to rabbits almost give one the impression that the Isle of Wight was one large warren from which considerable profit was derived.[20]

Tavistock Abbey had several warrens on its estates as well as a warren in the park close to the monastery, while Abingdon Abbey had a warren at Culham, the site of which is now occupied by Warren Farm and a wood called the Warren.[21] A warren was a highly-profitable adjunct to an estate, as can be seen from the estate accounts of Sir Thomas Tresham of Rushton (Nottinghamshire) in the mid-sixteenth century. On his estate at Misterton (Leicestershire) he derived a considerable part of his income from a warren in the park. A permanent warrener was employed, together with the occasional services of a man to mend the nets and snares. In 1551 the total expenditure was about £10 0s 0d, while the income from the sale of rabbits and skins came to £130 13s 2d or about 22 per cent of the total income of the estate. Rabbits continued to form an important part of the economy of Tresham's estate; the warren at Rushton was 12ha (30 acres) in extent, and there was another warren or 'connegerie' on his land at Pipewell. Ferrets were kept for bolting the

**3** *Medieval illustration of rabbit-catching. Rabbits made a valuable contribution to manorial income and many estates maintained warrens in which the delicate rabbits were carefully nurtured and guarded.*

rabbits from their artificially constructed burrows, and three times each week in the season carriers journeyed to London with rabbits and skins, and contracts were made with London poulterers guaranteeing a regular supply.

In 1636 the warrener on the Lulworth Castle estate in Dorset belonging to the Earl of Suffolk was paid 1s 0d per couple for 112 couple of rabbits. The Marquess of Salisbury's accounts for Cranborne (Dorset) for the same period list several profitable warrens established on the poor soils there, including one kept by a blind man 'Old Joe Seaborowe' and another leased for £12 a year to a warrener who was obliged to maintain a breeding stock of at least 200 rabbits.[22] Rabbits continued to be highly-prized and pampered creatures, incapable of making their own burrows, and in 1652 several people were accused of poaching on a warren at Badbury Rings (Dorset) and not only taking 200 coneys but also of destroying 18 coney burrows so that the remaining rabbits died for lack of shelter.

Various methods of taking the rabbits were employed by warreners (Fig. 3), the most common being with ferrets and nets.[23] On many estates breeding stock was exchanged between friends and neighbours. For example, in 1582 Sir Charles Somerset wrote from Monmouthshire to Matthew

Smyth of Long Ashton near Bristol to ask for some breeding rabbits from his warren

as many doe conyes as convenyently you can spare, not predjudicing your game, the most black if you have any store, which doing you shall minister unto me an acceptable pleasure . . .[24]

The sandy soils of the Breckland in Norfolk and Suffolk were ideally suited to the production of rabbits and several thousand acres were occupied by warrens, often surrounded by a high bank. Many also contained a lodge or house for the warrener and his family. A good example of such a lodge survives as a small tower at Thetford which dates from the fifteenth century and provided a storehouse with living accommodation above for the warrener. From his high dwelling he could survey the warren and protect the rabbits from poachers, either human or animal. It is situated within the former park which belonged to the wealthy Augustinian priory of Thetford.

Hares were also carefully protected for both food and sport on medieval estates, but since they live entirely above ground their conservation has left little evidence in the landscape except for the 'hare warren' place-names which survive on estates all over the country. These refer to the second meaning of the word 'warren' and denote places in which landowners or others had been granted by the Crown rights of hunting or *free warren*. Such free warrens were frequently used for a variety of sporting purposes and the following account of lengthy proceedings in the court of King's Bench in 1377 suggests that parts were also used for arable and grazing land. The case concerned trespass by a dozen named men upon the free warren belonging to the Dean and Chapter of Wells at North Curry (Somerset). The canons appear to have wildly exaggerated the value of the game and the extent of their losses, for they claimed that men had taken fish, hares, conies, pheasants and partridges amounting to the unbelievably large sum of £200, and had also damaged the grazing and trampled the corn growing there to the value of £40, as well as taking timber and brushwood, and beating and threatening the servants. Similarly in 1372, it was alleged that certain named persons had broken into the Duke of Lancaster's park and warren at Higham Ferrers (Northamptonshire), where the remains of the former castle and park survive on the north side of the church. They were said to have carried away deer, hares, conies, pheasants and partridges.[25]

Within parks and warrens, lodges or houses for the park keeper or warrener were frequently constructed, many with moats for protection. These, or their sites, often survive as additional evidence of former parks, and retain names such as warren house or park lodge. At Beckley Park (Oxfordshire) the site of the lodge built by Richard, Earl of Cornwall in *c.*1230 survives, defended by three concentric moats. A drawing of 1589 shows the lodge in Groveley Forest (Wiltshire) as a substantial house surrounded by a wooden pale with deer grazing within the enclosure. The remains of similar lodges, often with complex defences or moats, survive within the former parks at Alvechurch

(Worcestershire), Writtle (Essex) and Gillingham (Dorset).

Dovecots were also a feature of medieval estates, since the right to keep doves or pigeons, which are voracious feeders, was confined to lords of manors whose pigeons were exceedingly unpopular with the tenants upon whose crops they fed. Dovecots or 'culver houses' survive in many estates and in numerous place-names. Pigeons provided a supply of fresh meat throughout the year, and were a useful supplement to the restricted medieval diet; their rich dung made a good manure for gardens. Kept in dovecots with a ladder, or for circular buildings a 'potence' – a revolving stairway mounted on a central pivot, the birds could conveniently be caught and brought fresh to the kitchen. Although they were so common, and in spite of the fact that there are hundreds of surviving examples, dovecots rarely figure in manorial surveys or accounts and little detail is available concerning their management and profitability. The size and elaborate nature of the surviving dovecots (Fig. 4), many containing several hundred nest holes, and the substantial manner in which they are built is an indication of their importance on many medieval estates, and the fact that they were the jealously-guarded prerogative of lords of the manor makes them a good indicator of seigneurial control of the manorial economy.

Church estates also possessed dovecots, and the accounts of Tavistock Abbey, for example, include numerous references to them. Dovecots are to be found in the chambers above the chancels of parish churches at Compton Martin (Somerset) and Elkstone (Gloucestershire), as well as in the monastic buildings at Hinton Charterhouse (Somerset). Many monastic barns included dovecots either as free-standing buildings or as part of the barn itself. Most manorial lords possessed this valuable perquisite, and fine examples

**4**  *Dovecot at Willington (Bedfordshire). Beside the manor house of the Gostwick family, the large size and solid construction are a reminder of the importance of pigeons in the late-medieval manorial economy.*

survive at Minster Lovell (Oxfordshire), Cotehele (Cornwall), Higham Castle (Northamptonshire) and Garway (Herefordshire), the latter, on a manor belonging to the Knights Hospitallers, consisting of a substantial circular building with an inscription recording that it was built in 1326. The resentment felt by manorial tenants towards the lord's pigeons is evident from the fact that among the causes of the rebellion in Norfolk led by Robert Ket in 1549 the keeping of pigeons by landowners and the damage caused to crops both by pigeons and by the rabbits from manorial warrens were both listed by the rebels among their complaints.[26]

Mills were also a valuable manorial perquisite. They were expensive to build and maintain, and most manorial custumals required tenants to abandon any hand-querns and to have their corn ground at the manorial mill, leaving a proportion as toll-corn. Domesday Book records a large number of mills all over the country, wherever a suitable stream could be channelled and harnessed to provide the motive power. For example there were 304 mills in Norfolk, 256 in Lincolnshire and 161 in Northamptonshire. A century later windmills began to make their appearance, again as a manorial monopoly. How common mills became as features of the later medieval landscape is attested by their incorporation into so many place-names, by the number of leats and mounds which survive as earthworks, and by the number of water-mills and windmills on paintings and bench-ends in medieval churches.[27]

# 2 The later Middle Ages

The fourteenth century saw the end of the long period of expansion in population, settlements, arable land, towns, trade and monasteries. Instead there followed decades of population decline, frequent poor harvests, recurrent plagues which reached a peak but did not end with the Black Death of 1348–9, of retreat from marginal lands and abandonment of settlements. There was also a decline in the fervour of monasticism and in the popularity of the religious orders, as men concentrated upon individual salvation through the foundation of chantries and the costly extension and adornment of parish churches. Many estates, both lay and ecclesiastical, abandoned the direct farming of their own lands, leasing farms or even whole manors to tenants and commuting labour services for payments in money or kind. But despite the destructive horror of the Black Death and subsequent plagues, and notwithstanding famines and civil strife, there was wealth enough for the more fortunate or enterprising sections of society and this wealth was reflected in a demand for more comfort in their houses and greater elegance in their surroundings.

Castles became increasingly elaborate, both as defences and residences and, even more important, as status symbols in the landscape, demonstrating the opulence of their occupants and their power over their tenantry. Rising standards and increasing expectations of comfort and privacy led many gentry families to build fortified manor houses whose fortifications served for display rather than fulfilling any serious military purpose. A very early example is Stokesay Castle (Shropshire) which was built with large windows and without serious defences, apart from a moat and gatehouse, as early as 1280. Later examples are to be found all over the country, and include Nunney Castle (Somerset), Sir John Fastolf's impressive Caister Castle (Norfolk) or Tattershall Castle (Lincolnshire) built by Ralph, Lord Cromwell in the mid-fifteenth century. This was obviously intended for show rather than defence in spite of its tower, battlements and moat, which would have overawed the peasantry of the surrounding flat fenland countryside. It also emphasized Cromwell's importance and would have been effective against any local insurrection, but could have hardly resisted a determined attack by a large and expert force. Likewise, the moated Herstmonceux Castle (East Sussex) was built in c. 1440 by Sir Roger de Fiennes with extensive use of brick; it was designed as an elegant country house incorporating every luxury which the period could offer.

Another example of the new-style castle is Bodiam (East Sussex) and again, in spite of its moat and massive towers, it was built to provide comfort and convenience; an early twentieth-century owner of Bodiam, Lord Curzon, declared that 'Whether for Sport or Dalliance, or more serious affairs, Whether for a life of pleasure or hazard or war, Bodiam castle was equally well placed'.[1]

In the interests of the privacy and convenience of the owners, dwellings had also to be provided for officers of the household, like the range of houses surrounding the courtyard at Dartington (Devon), the never-completed, ruined Kirby Muxloe (Leicestershire) or Coughton Court (Warwickshire).

Increasing wealth and leisure also led to developments in the surroundings of castles and manor houses, including the construction of bowling greens, tilt yards, walks, summer-houses and prospect bowers, and the creation of gardens designed purely for pleasure rather than for the production of food and herbs (Fig. 5). At Kenilworth Castle, for example, the late-medieval amenities included walks laid out around the huge lake or mere, which was overlooked by the castle and formed part of its defences, and a 'plaisaunce' or pleasure ground laid out by Henry V in *c.* 1414 and provided with a timber-framed banqueting house. Raglan Castle on the Welsh border also had fine gardens, which by the sixteenth century included terraces, flower-beds, borders, fountains and sculpture.

Another late-medieval development, the primary object of which was to emphasize status, was the construction of manor houses with moats. Many hundreds of moated houses were created in areas such as north Warwickshire, Worcestershire, Suffolk, Cambridgeshire and north-west

**5**   *Wardour Castle (Wiltshire). Built by John, Lord Lovell at the end of the fourteenth century, the castle later passed into the hands of the Arundell family. It was besieged and partly demolished during the Civil War, and the ruins became a romantic feature in the grounds of the Georgian mansion built nearby for the eighth Lord Arundell.*

Essex, where water and a retentive clay subsoil were available. As well as providing evidence of the importance and separation of the inhabitants, moated sites did give some measure of security during a long period of lawlessness and civil war. They were also useful for drainage, for sewage disposal and as fishponds, but without the status they conferred it is unlikely that quite so many people would have gone to the enormous labour and expense of creating them.[2]

## Medieval gardens

The gardens on most medieval estates were intended to provide the household with vegetables, fruit and herbs, and few detailed records survive of the modest expenditure required for such mundane functions. One of the earliest depictions of a garden is in the elaborate plan of Christ Church, Canterbury, made in *c.*1165 to show the sophisticated system of water supply and drainage which the monks enjoyed. The plan also shows a herb garden with rows of plants and a trellis fence, as well as a vineyard and orchard outside the precincts. The accounts of Beaulieu Abbey (Hampshire) during the thirteenth century include expenditure on the kitchen and herb garden and show that the garden produced apples, cider, honey and hemp, as well as cereals and beans. During the fourteenth century the abbey gardens at Glastonbury produced beans, leeks, onions, garlic, apples, pears and various herbs, as well as hemp, flax, madder and wine from the vineyard. Above all, very large quantities of garlic were produced, since it was useful to add flavour to an otherwise dull meal and was also highly regarded as a health-giving and beneficial addition to the diet.[3]

Other accounts make incidental references to cabbages, kale, carrots, radish and peas, and it is clear that the growing of such vegetables in small plots by all sections of medieval society was widespread, although few felt it necessary to make any record of such commonplace activity. Wealthy landowners, however, could afford the expense of laying out elaborate pleasure-gardens on their estates, but since gardens are peculiarly subject both to neglect and to alteration at the dictates of changing fashion, none have survived unchanged from the Middle Ages and we are mainly dependent on documentary evidence for knowledge of their form. During the early twelfth century the royal accounts reveal that Henry I had gardens at Windsor, Dunstable and Havering as well as at Woodstock where he also maintained a collection of exotic animals including lions, lynxes, leopards, camels and a porcupine. Henry II laid out extensive pleasure and herb gardens at the royal palace of Clarendon near Salisbury, enclosed by walls and containing lawns, walks, fishponds, trees and benches. At Woodstock, Henry II created Rosamund's Bower for his mistress, Rosamund Clifford, and Henry III added further gardens, walks, pools, fountains and summer-houses.

During the later thirteenth century the manor of Harlestone (Northamptonshire) was acquired by the royal official, Henry de Bray, who proceeded to reorganize the estate and lay out a garden there during the 1290s. His garden included a walled herb garden, a series of walks with flower borders, a bower, a grassy mound, seats, a pond, fountain and a dovecot.[4] Some monastic gardens also produced flowers as well as herbs and vegetables, and were obviously intended as pleasure gardens. One example is the garden at the Hampshire nunnery of Wherwell which was laid out along the bank of the river Test and described as 'a place set apart for the refreshment of the soul'.

Private gardens were an essential feature of each cell in a Carthusian monastery, and each monk was expected to spend some time on the cultivation of his small plot. The well-preserved ruins of the former

Carthusian house at Mount Grace in North Yorkshire show the gardens behind each of the dwellings, as well as revealing the substantial size of each 'cell' or house provided for the individual monks. The Benedictine monks at Durham in the fifteenth century had a garden and a bowling green. It should of course be remembered that monastic flower gardens were not entirely frivolous, for some of the plants and flowers could be used for medicinal purposes or to provide the raw materials from which illuminators produced their colours. Gardening was a particularly suitable activity for monks and nuns, since as well as giving innocent and useful exercise, it did not interfere with the regular performance of the offices. Moreover the Scriptures are full of references to gardens and gardening, from the first garden established in Eden by the Almighty and the vineyard planted by Noah, through all the gardening similes of the Song of Songs, to the passion of Christ in the garden of Gethsemane, the burial in a garden and the first appearance to Mary Magdalene after the Resurrection which took place in the garden, 'and she supposing him to be the gardener . . .'. This scene in the garden, with the women at the empty tomb and the dramatic encounter between the Risen Christ and Mary Magdalene is depicted in a stained glass window of *c.*1500 at Fairford (Gloucestershire) and shows the large garden in the background, stretching away into the distance.

## Church estates in the medieval landscape

As one of the major landowners of medieval England, the impact of the Church upon the landscape was naturally very great. The estates of bishops, cathedral chapters and the great religious houses ranked alongside those of the greatest of lay landowners. Like their lay neighbours, the churchmen administered their estates to produce food, profit and status. Bishops and abbots possessed manor houses, deer parks, fishponds and warrens, and were as quick as other landlords to exploit resources such as mills, building stone or minerals on their lands. Most obviously of course, the Church dominated the landscape with its great cathedrals, huge monastic houses and some 12,000 parish churches and chapelries, so that there were few places which were far from the sight of a church and everywhere the sound of church bells could be heard.

Another distinctive imprint of the Church estates survives in the form of outlying farms or granges, barns and inns. Since lands once acquired by an ecclesiastical institution were likely to remain in Church hands in perpetuity, the administrators of Church estates could afford to take a long view of capital investments, so that granges, farms and barns and other buildings are frequently built to a very high standard.

An early example of an ecclesiastical landlord imposing his own ideas upon his estates is Roger de Caen, bishop of Salisbury 1107–39, and Chancellor of England. Among his widespread lands, castles and manor houses, Bishop Roger was particularly fond of his estate at Sherborne (Dorset), where he built a magnificent castle, with moat, curtain walls, lofty towers and an impressive keep. He also gave thought to his own comfort, and within the keep he provided comfortable rooms overlooking a cloistered courtyard. Around the castle he enclosed a large deer park, laid out an orchard and vineyard, and contrived a series of fishponds along the shallow valley

6 *Estates of Abingdon Abbey. The map gives an indication of the extent of the estates of a typical rich Benedictine abbey with large ancient endowments of land. (J. Bond.)*

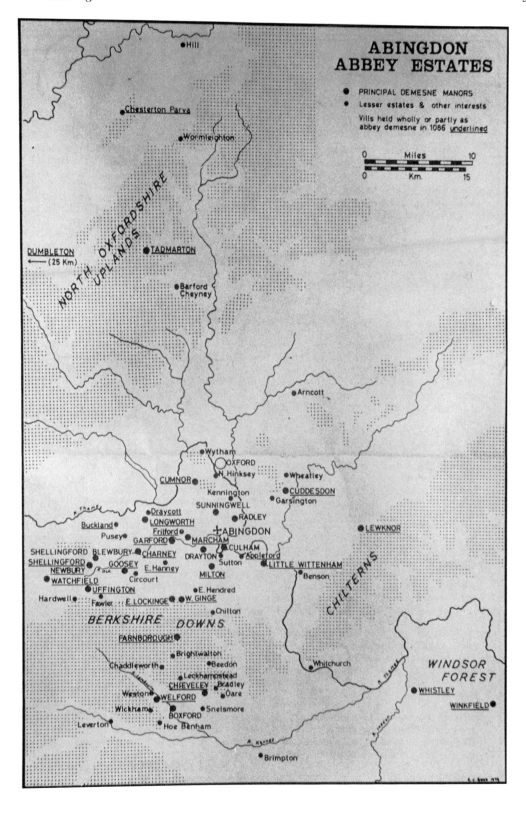

ABINGDON
ABBEY ESTATES

● PRINCIPAL DEMESNE MANORS
● Lesser estates & other interests

Vills held wholly or partly as
abbey demesne in 1086 underlined

Miles  0 — 10
Km.  0 — 15

●Hill

●Chesterton Parva

●Wormleighton

NORTH OXFORDSHIRE UPLANDS

DUMBLETON
←— (25 Km.)

●TADMARTON

●Barford Cheyney

●Arncott

●Wytham
○OXFORD
●N. Hinksey
CUMNOR●
●Wheatley
●Kennington
CUDDESDON●
SUNNINGWELL●
●Garsington
Draycott●
LONGWORTH●
●RADLEY
Buckland●
Frilford●
LEWKNOR
Pusey●
●ABINGDON
GARFORD●
MARCHAM●
SHELLINGFORD BLEWBURY●
CHARNEY●
●CULHAM
DRAYTON●
●Appleford
SHELLINGFORD●
GOOSEY●
Sutton●
LITTLE WITTENHAM●
NEWBURY
E. Hanney●
●Benson
●WATCHFIELD
Circourt●
MILTON
UFFINGTON●
●E. Hendred
Hardwell● Fawler●
E.LOCKINGE●
●W. GINGE
●Chilton

CHILTERNS

BERKSHIRE DOWNS

FARNBOROUGH●
●Brightwalton
Chaddleworth●
●Beedon
●Whitchurch
●Leckhampstead
CHIEVELEY●
●Bradley
Weston●
WELFORD●
●Oare
Wickham●
●Snelsmore
BOXFORD●
Leverton●
●Hoe Benham

WINDSOR FOREST

●WHISTLEY

WINKFIELD●

●Brimpton

of the river Yeo. To the monks of the nearby Benedictine abbey he granted every tenth skin from the deer killed within his park to be used for the binding of their books, permission to take venison from the park for important guests or for sick monks, and licence to fish in his stew ponds upon four occasions in the year 'with nets and other engines'. The monks could also graze four cows and four calves within the deer park. Bishop Roger of Salisbury also built a magnificent castle on his Wiltshire estates at Malmesbury and at Devizes, where he created a deer park of which the formidable bank is still clearly visible.[5]

The ancient abbey of Abingdon derived its income from an estate which may be seen as typical of many other Benedictine houses (Fig. 6). Most of the abbey's extensive lands centred around Abingdon itself, the Thames valley, the Vale of the White Horse and the Berkshire Downs. Nearby lands were used for orchards, gardens and a vineyard, while other estates produced cereals, butter and cheese or concentrated on the production of wool. Woodland in east Berkshire produced timber and pigs. The abbey also possessed a deer park, fishponds, fisheries along the Thames, stone quarries, water-mills and a rabbit warren. Scattered across the manors were more than a dozen manor houses, used as residences for the abbot, retirement homes or rest houses, and several manors also possessed barns where the abbey produce could be stored, as well as their own dovecots, fishponds and warrens.[6]

In the south-east the great monastic houses of Christ Church, Canterbury, Battle Abbey and St Augustine's Priory specialized in arable farming on their lands, especially in the production of barley, and the huge aisled barns which were built to store their produce are still notable features of the landscape. The medieval barn at Frindsbury (Kent) which belonged to Christ Church priory is 52.5m (172ft) long, while the barn at Alciston (Sussex) on the lands of

**7** *Abbots' Kitchen, Glastonbury Abbey (Somerset). This huge late fourteenth-century kitchen which served the abbots' separate establishment provides an indication of the magnificent life-style enjoyed by Benedictine abbots whose vast estates placed them among the wealthiest of late-medieval landowners.*

Battle Abbey is 52m (170ft) long and is part of a fine set of medieval buildings, including a manor house and a dovecot.[7]

Glastonbury Abbey, the richest of all the English monasteries, had estates scattered across southern England, but especially in Somerset, Dorset and Wiltshire. The abbot's kitchen (Fig. 7), which survives so dramatically amid the ruins at Glastonbury, is a reminder of the splendour in which the late-medieval abbots lived. The commissioners at the Dissolution reported

**8** *Fountains Abbey (Yorkshire). The massive remains show clearly the enormous building programme which had gone on throughout the Middle Ages, and how the wealth derived from the widespread monastic estates was spent.*

The house is great and goodly, and so princely as we have not seen the like; with 4 parks adjoining . . . [and] 4 fair manor places.

Farther afield the abbot of Glastonbury possessed many more manor houses, including a fine stone-built house at Ashbury (Berkshire), with a hall, well-appointed chambers, numerous fireplaces and every comfort and convenience, including a first-floor indoor lavatory. Under the notable abbot, Michael of Amesbury (1235–52), the area under cultivation was greatly extended, lands were reclaimed from the sea along the Somerset coast, marshes were drained, fields were enclosed, new barns, sheep-houses, dovecots and dairies were built, and stock increased until there were 1400 cattle and over 7000 sheep. The large estate was closely controlled from Glastonbury, and the bailiffs on each manor rendered detailed accounts each year.[8] The monks of the well-endowed cathedral priory of Durham possessed a holiday home at Finchale on the river Wear, downstream from Durham, where in a comfortable, rural retreat they could enjoy a break from the monotonous routine of their life at the cathedral.[9]

While the Benedictine monasteries operated within the framework of the manorial system, with the abbey as manorial lord and the lands farmed by tenants, the Cistercians, who began to found houses in England from the early twelfth century, sought remote sites and farmed their own lands through their system of lay-brothers. The wealth of the great Cistercian abbeys in the north of England was based on their vast sheep flocks on the moors. During the thirteenth century Fountains Abbey had up to 18,000 sheep on Malham Moor and thousands more elsewhere in the Dales (Fig. 8). Meaux Abbey had 11,000 sheep and 1000 beasts in Holderness.[10] On the lands of the abbeys of south-west England the sheep flocks were regularly moved long distances between different manors. Wool from the Beaulieu Abbey sheep flocks in Berkshire was brought back to the *Bergerie* or wool store at Beaulieu where it was washed, graded and packed for the market. From the *Bergerie* the sheep flocks at all the distant granges were controlled and managed.[11]

In the mid-twelfth century the Mowbray family granted to the Cistercian abbey which they had endowed at Byland, grazing rights for sheep and cattle throughout their large Chase of Nidderdale. Interestingly the Mowbrays reserved the hunting for themselves and stipulated that the deer were not to be disturbed and that no monastic swine should be allowed on the Chase during the midsummer period so as not to molest or destroy the new-born fawns.[12]

With their huge estates spreading over so many square miles of moorland, it is hardly surprising that the Cistercians developed a system of granges or outlying farms and during the thirteenth and fourteenth centuries these were worked by lay-brothers with the help of some hired labour. At first the granges were simple buildings providing merely sleeping and eating facilities, but during the later Middle Ages many granges were rebuilt in stone and resembled small manor houses, often with a chapel, barn and other buildings. Surviving remains and earthworks of former Cistercian granges such as Cayton, Morker, Kilgram or Linton in Yorkshire, St Leonard's (Hampshire), Musden (Staffordshire), Burton-on-the-Wold (Leicestershire) or Haseley on the Isle of Wight show that by the end of the Middle Ages these granges included substantial buildings, often with a moated manor house, large barn and houses for the labourers.[13] A good example of a Cistercian grange survives at Great Coxwell (Berkshire), which served as the centre for the extensive estates around Faringdon, belonging to the distant abbey of Beaulieu (Hampshire). The huge barn, 46m (152ft) long and 15.5m (51ft) high (Fig. 9), built in an elaborate and sophisticated fashion during the thirteenth century, was used to store the produce of the monks' estates before it was taken to local markets or on the long journey to Beaulieu. The permanent staff on the grange at Great Coxwell included eight ploughmen, two carters, a hayward, forester, baker, cheese-maker, porter, swineherd, cook, kitchen boy, cowherd and three shepherds.[14]

Other monastic orders also had outlying farmsteads worked by monastic servants and often also serving as lodging houses for the abbot or rest-houses for the monks. The sites of these former monastic properties are often distinguished by their large stone-built medieval barns, many of them of enormous size and clearly part of the estate of extremely wealthy and confident institutions. Examples include the two barns, the Barley barn and the Wheat barn, built during the early Middle Ages at Temple Cressing (Essex) on the estate which until 1312 belonged to the Knights Templars and then passed to the Knights Hospitallers. Fine granges and barns also survive on the former estates of many other monastic houses such as those at Ashleworth and Frocester (Gloucestershire) or Bradford-on-

Avon (Wiltshire). The last belonged to the nuns of the wealthy nunnery at Shaftesbury (Dorset), and they also possessed the grange at Tisbury where many of the medieval buildings survive, including the thatched-roofed barn which is 64 m (210ft) long.

Cathedral and monastic establishments also gained substantial income from the crowds of pilgrims attracted to worship at their shrines or to seek spiritual benefit from the innumerable relics whose power the monks so assiduously promoted. For the accommodation of these pilgrims numerous inns and hostelries were provided. Surviving examples include the Angel and Royal Hotel at Grantham, one of the finest of all English medieval inns which belonged to the Hospitallers, the New Inn at Gloucester built for pilgrims by St Peter's Abbey in *c*.1457, the George at Norton St Philip (Somerset) (Fig. 10) built by the Carthusians of nearby Hinton Charterhouse, the aptly-named Shaven Crown at Shipton-under-Wychwood (Oxfordshire) which belonged to the Cistercian monks of Bruern, or the two twelfth-century hostelries for pilgrims which remain at Canterbury: the North Hall and Eastbridge Hospital. For more adventurous pilgrims undertaking journeys to continental Europe or even to the Holy Land itself, parts of the thirteenth-century

**9** *Great Coxwell barn, near Faringdon. This huge thirteenth-century barn served the estates around Faringdon, which had been given by King John to the Cistercian monks of Beaulieu Abbey in Hampshire. The stone-built barn is 46m (152ft) long and 15.5m (51ft) high; its impressive size and solid construction are remarkable witness to the immense wealth and widespread estates of the medieval monastic houses.*

**10** *The George Inn, Norton St Philip (Somerset). This late-medieval inn was part of the estate of the Carthusian monks at Hinton Charterhouse, and was used as a guest-house and for the sale of wool and cloth.*

Maison Dieu survive at Dover and of God's House at Southampton.

The profits from monastic estates and the income derived from pilgrims went to fund the building of even larger churches and cloisters, complete with elaborate decorations and rich furnishings. The greater monasteries, secure in the knowledge of their long history and vast wealth, vied with each other in the magnificence of their buildings, the opulence of their churches, the splendour of their treasures and the capacity of their barns. Even the Cistercians joined the general trend, regardless of St Bernard's

puritanical condemnation of outward show and his bitter remark that

For God's sake, if men are not ashamed of these follies, why at least do they not shrink from the expense?

## The church and agricultural improvement

The medieval church made a significant impact upon the landscape in two other ways. In the attempt to increase the income from their estates, cathedrals and monasteries were at the forefront of land reclamation projects, drainage schemes and industrial undertakings; and in its encouragement of individual charity and care for the poor the Church promoted the foundation of innumerable almshouses, schools, hospitals, guilds and fraternities.

In the north of England the monastic houses played a major part in land reclamation and improvement, in the extension of settlements and in the huge expansion of sheep farming during the Middle Ages. It was the cathedrals and monastic houses which possessed the capital and the long-term interest to take the lead in the farming advances of the thirteenth century, and churchmen like Prior Henry Eastry of Christ Church, Canterbury extended their lands, invested heavily in farm buildings, mills, land drainage and soil improvement. By the early fourteenth century the monks of Christ Church had more than 8000 acres under cultivation. In the Fens and the Somerset Levels it was the great monastic houses like Crowland, Peterborough or Ramsey (in eastern England) or Glastonbury, Muchelney and Athelney (in the west), which had the wealth and impetus to engage in major drainage projects. In the Romney Marsh area of Kent the sea defences and water courses still bear the names of medieval archbishops of Canterbury, and the monasteries played a leading part in the reclamation of large areas around the Wash and in Holderness.

The monasteries were also active throughout the later Middle Ages in developing the industrial and mineral potential of their estates, with lead mining in Somerset, Derbyshire and Yorkshire, coal mining in Nottinghamshire, Derbyshire and Durham, ironstone mining and smelting in Yorkshire, tin mining on Dartmoor and salt production in Cheshire as well as at various places along the coast. It was also the monasteries which possessed the capital to develop stone quarries on their estates.

The abbeys of Crowland, Ramsey, Peterborough and Bury St Edmunds all had quarrying rights at Barnack (Northamptonshire), in Somerset the stone quarries at Doulting were exploited by the cathedral at Wells and by the monks at Glastonbury, the Chilmark quarries in Wiltshire were developed to supply stone for Salisbury cathedral, and it was for use in churches all over England that the quarries of Purbeck (Dorset) and the alabaster quarries of the Trent and Dove valleys in Derbyshire and Nottinghamshire were developed.[15]

The proprietary chapels and chantries attached to many parish churches and the monuments and brasses which dominate so many medieval chancels are a reminder of the rights over parish churches which continued to be possessed by the lords of the manor. Stanton Harcourt church (Oxfordshire), Lowick (Northamptonshire) or Cobham (Kent) were filled with monuments; these monuments have turned the churches into mausoleums for the Harcourts, Greenes and Cobhams respectively, and in other churches also the late-medieval parishioners found themselves confronted in church by the massive memorials to those who had previously ruled over all aspects of their secular lives. The church of St Mary at Warwick was rebuilt in the most lavish style by the earls of Warwick, and the Beauchamp chapel with its sumptuous tomb to Richard Beauchamp, Earl of Warwick, who died in 1439, is a magnificent example of late-medieval English architecture and craftsmanship. The Fitzherberts, who were lords of Norbury (Derbyshire), rebuilt the church on the grandest scale and filled it with their monuments.

Inscriptions also provide evidence of the part played by manorial lords in the extension, alteration or furnishing of late-medieval churches. The stone screen at Bunbury church (Cheshire) bears the message 'This chapel was made at the cost and charge of Sir Raufe Egerton Knight in the year of our Lord God MCCCCC & XXVII'. At Lavenham (Suffolk) the arms of the lord of the manor, John de Vere, Earl of Oxford, are prominently carved on the church as a tribute to his contribution to the late-medieval rebuilding work, while long inscriptions invite prayers for the souls of the Branch and Spring families, the wealthy clothiers who built the two chapels on either side of the church during the early sixteenth century. Nearby, the church at Long Melford has numerous inscriptions recording the generosity of those who contributed to the building during the fifteenth century, notably the Clopton and Martyn families, who were the most prominent landowners.

## Charitable foundations

It was the Church which fostered the foundation of the most characteristic endowments of the later Middle Ages: chantries, colleges, hospitals, almshouses and schools. For the wealthy founders such institutions provided a practical, public demonstration of religious piety, and combined spiritual benefit and worldly prestige with a genuine benevolence towards the less fortunate. The hospital of St Cross in Winchester was founded by Bishop Henry of Blois, brother of King Stephen, in 1136, and the massive church was begun soon afterwards; the attractive hospital buildings which survive, with their communal dining hall and range of individual lodgings for bedesmen, were constructed during the mid-fifteenth century. Winchester also possesses the school established by William of Wykeham in the late fourteenth century. At Tong (Shropshire) Elizabeth, widow of Sir Fulke de Pembrugge, founded a college of chantry priests in 1410. She ordered that the college

should consist of a warden and four priests, two clerks and 13 poor persons, who were to live in common and maintain a constant round of services for the souls of the founder and her family. To accommodate the new college, the church was almost entirely rebuilt, and college buildings were erected around a quadrangle, south of the church. The collegiate buildings have been demolished, but the elaborate choir stalls of the chantry priests remain in the chancel. The rest of the interior is crowded with the tombs and memorials of the later owners of Tong, the Vernon family, who added an elegant chantry chapel with beautiful fan-vaulting on the south side of the church.

Among innumerable other examples of such charitable institutions, the late-medieval hospital established in Stamford (Lincolnshire) by the wealthy merchant, William Browne, remains as one of the best examples in England, while at Abingdon, the charming terrace of almshouses founded as Christ's Hospital in 1446 survives in the churchyard of St Helen's parish church. By the end of the Middle Ages few towns were without similar philanthropic endowments, ranging in size from small almshouses or doles of food or money, to hospitals like St Leonards at York, which in the mid-thirteenth century could accommodate more than two hundred people.

Two of the best preserved and attractive examples of late-medieval charity survive at Ewelme (Oxfordshire) and Sherborne (Dorset). At Ewelme (Fig. 11) during the 1430s Alice, grand-daughter of Geoffrey Chaucer, and her husband William de la Pole, Duke of Suffolk, rebuilt the parish

---

11   *Ornate tomb of Alice, Duchess of Suffolk, Ewelme church (Oxfordshire). She died in 1475 and her fine tomb is situated close to the altar. Above is her effigy displayed with all her finery, while below she is shown as an emaciated corpse, deprived of all wordly possessions.*

---

**12** *Tattershall Castle (Lincolnshire). Built by Ralph, Lord Cromwell c.1440. The keep is 34m (110ft) high and dominates the surrounding Fenland countryside.*

church and beside it founded an almshouse for 13 poor men under the spiritual oversight of two chaplains, and a school for the village children where they were to be taught 'freely, without exaction of any schole hire'. All three institutions continue to be used for their original purpose. At Sherborne in 1437 money was raised by local people to found the Hospital of St John the Baptist and St John the Evangelist to accommodate 'twelve pore feeble and ympotent men and four old women'. A matron and a chaplain were appointed to attend to their bodily and spiritual needs, and the residents were expected to hear Mass every day in the chapel which formed part of the establishment. The hospital is still used for its original purpose, although it was considerably enlarged during the nineteenth century.[16]

Another example of a self-sufficient late-medieval complex established by a wealthy landowner with total control of every aspect of life within his estate was at Tattershall (Lincolnshire) (Fig. 12). Here in the fifteenth century, Ralph, Lord Cromwell, who held the office of Treasurer of England under

**13** *Hindon (Wiltshire). The wide street of the planned town created in c.1220 on the estate of the Bishop of Winchester.*

Henry VI, built Tattershall Castle with its great brick keep 34m (110ft) high dominating the Fenland landscape. Lord Cromwell also built the nearby church on the grandest scale and regardless of expense, endowed a college of priests to conduct the services and to serve his chantry foundation, established almshouses and a grammar school and fostered the growth of the adjacent town, securing a market and building a market cross.

The creation of new towns inhabited by craftsmen and burgesses was a profitable late-medieval enterprise, and landowners, both lay and ecclesiastical, fostered such developments on their estates. Such 'planted' towns are often recognizable by their regular plan, wide streets and large market places. The new town of Salisbury was established in 1219 by Bishop Richard Poore and laid out with a grid pattern of streets in the meadows below the original settlement and cathedral at Old Sarum. Henry II founded Market Harborough (Leicestershire) on the manor of Great Bowden in the late twelfth century;

Kingston upon Hull (Yorkshire) was established by Edward I on his royal manor during the late thirteenth century. Chipping Sodbury (Gloucestershire) was founded as a completely new town on his estate by William le Gras in 1218, the place-name element 'Chipping', meaning market, gives a clue to its origin, as does its single broad street widening into a market place with the burgess plots on either side. The bishops of Winchester were energetic in the creation of new towns as speculative ventures on their estates (Fig. 13). One of the most successful was New Alresford (Hampshire), founded in the thirteenth century by Bishop Godfrey de Lucy. A charter was obtained from King John granting the right to markets and fairs, and in order to attract burgesses to his new town the bishop provided a fulling mill, a market hall, a communal oven, and most spectacularly, built a great dam across the river Alre to give a powerful head of water for driving other mills, 'one of the largest secular earthworks surviving from medieval England'.[17]

# 3 New men, new money and new ideas in the sixteenth century

The coming of the Tudor dynasty in 1485 and with it the ending of the long period of warfare, civil strife and dynastic uncertainty which had marked the later Middle Ages meant that houses and estates could now be planned without considerations of defence. In addition, the political, economic and religious changes of the early Tudor decades ensured that many of the aristocracy and gentry had large, disposable incomes to spend as they pleased upon their estates and upon architectural extravagance. The sixteenth century witnessed an outburst of building as all over the country landowners built new houses designed to display their wealth and taste, to amaze or infuriate their neighbours and to provide new standards of comfort for themselves and their families. The Tudor dynasty provided strong government and opportunities for courtiers, office-holders and royal officials to acquire immense wealth, while increasing population, rising rentals and improved prices for foodstuffs and wool, as well as the scope for enrichment provided by the dispersal of the former monastic lands, all meant that landowners could afford to indulge their ideas as never before.

Wealth which in an earlier age would have served to found a hospital, endow a charity or rebuild part of a parish church, and to provide for the well-being of the donor's soul in the next life, could now be used to ensure that his memory would live on through architectural grandeur or territorial extravagance. This passion for building extended from the aristocracy and gentry to merchants' houses in towns, manor houses in the country and to the farms of yeomen or freeholders.

Cold, uncomfortable and inconvenient, medieval castles no longer satisfied the demands for luxury and ease of living which sixteenth-century estate-owners could afford to indulge. When, early in the sixteenth century, Sir John Newton inherited Richmont Castle, the great stone-built fortress of the Gurney family at East Harptree (Somerset), he lost no time in demolishing it and building a modern house nearby. John Leland visited the place c. 1540 and commented that

Noble Gurney used to ly much at Richmonte Castle. Yt is now defacid to the hard ground, and Syr John Newton now lorde of it hath made his house harde by the ruines therof.

Sir John Newton could easily afford such extragavance, just as he could afford his enormous tomb in the parish church with the life-size effigies of himself and his wife, and around the base the figures of their eight sons and twelve daughters. During the early years of the sixteenth century a few buildings continued to be erected in the older style, such as Thornbury Castle (Gloucestershire) begun in 1511 by the Duke of Buckingham and still not finished when he was executed in 1521. But even this was a castle in name only and would hardly have

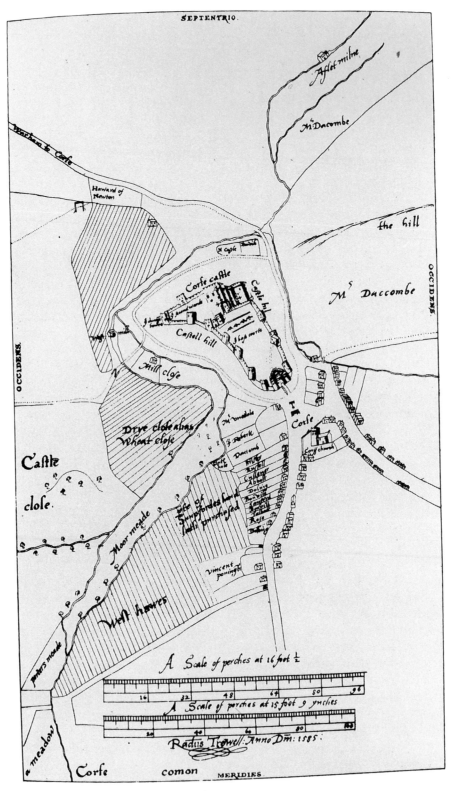

withstood a serious attack, and most contemporary buildings were beginning to show new features such as symmetrical fronts, large expanses of window, and much more attention to accommodation, comfort, sanitation and heating. Such houses included Layer Marney (Essex), The Vyne (Hampshire), Hengrave Hall (Suffolk), Compton Wynyates (Warwickshire), Stonyhurst (Lancashire) or Wolsey's great Hampton Court and the royal palaces built for Henry VIII at Nonsuch, Richmond and St James's Palace (Fig. 14).

Later came the numerous houses constructed out of former monasteries such as Lacock (Wiltshire), Titchfield (Hampshire), Newstead Abbey (Nottinghamshire), St Osyth's priory (Essex) or Buckland Abbey (Devon); while during the reign of Elizabeth the new and enormously expensive 'prodigy' houses, whose primary purpose was to display the wealth, status and taste of their owners, were built in great numbers – such as Longleat (Wiltshire), Holdenby (Northamptonshire), Burghley (Northamptonshire), Wollaton Hall (Nottinghamshire), Theobalds (Hertfordshire) or Bess of Hardwick's enormous mansion, Hardwick Hall (Derbyshire). In the north Lord Burghley's son, Thomas Cecil, rebuilt Snape Castle (Yorkshire) in 1587 and gave it the security of four strong corner towers in the older fashion; but in Yorkshire at the same period, Heslington Hall, Burton Constable Hall and Burton Agnes Hall were being built in the new symmetrical style with large windows and little thought for defence. Such houses were vast by the standards of any age. Sir

Christopher Hatton's house at Holdenby, for example, was comparable with the huge eighteenth-century monster houses at Blenheim and Castle Howard, and the impact upon the sixteenth-century landscape was all the greater because of the ebullient vulgarity, with profuse decoration of chimneys, turrets, pinnacles and parapets. Likewise, Audley End (Essex), built by Thomas Howard early in the seventeenth century, was the largest house of its time in England. There have been many architectural descriptions of this multitude of new style houses of the sixteenth century, but much less has been written about their surroundings, the elaborate gardens, walks, ornamental buildings, lakes, parks and the other features of the estates which were an essential accompaniment and background to the houses.

## Gardens

Gardens are among the most ephemeral of art forms. They are subject to change and rapid decay, or liable to be extensively altered or redesigned as fashions evolve, so that it is not easy to visualize the sort of garden which was thought desirable during the early sixteenth century. Three examples in the south-west of England, however, can serve to provide some clues, especially about the value attached to privacy within a garden. Shortly before the suppression of Glastonbury Abbey, the last abbot, Richard Whiting, then an old man, was described by one of the monks as seated in his private garden at the abbey during a summer morning in 1539, while in the nearby monastic church the monks were singing High Mass. The abbot was seated 'in an arbour of bay in the said garden' and in this secluded place was conducting a business transaction with a local gentleman.[1] The abbots of Glastonbury also had a garden beside their manor house at Mells (Somerset). During the early years of the

**14** *Plan of the town of Corfe Castle (Dorset) in 1585. This plan was drawn by Ralph Treswell and shows how the little town continued to be totally dominated by the great royal castle.*

sixteenth century a high wall was built around this garden to provide greater seclusion, with a terrace at the upper end and two mounds giving a view over the surrounding parkland.[2] At much the same time a walled garden was erected at Thornbury castle and the Duke of Buckingham's gardener, John Wynde, was employed to create

A goodly gardeyn to walk ynn closed with high walls imbattled . . . [and] a large and goodly orcharde full of younge grafftes well loden with frute, many roses and other pleasures; and in the same orcharde are many goodly alies to walk ynn oppenly.

John Wynde was described as 'diligent in making knots' – meaning intricately patterned beds with geometrically planned decoration and plantings. The Thornbury garden had a raised gallery or walkway from which the pattern of knots, perhaps arranged in heraldic or symbolic shapes, could be viewed to the best advantage (see also below).[3]

Tudor gentry wanted their gardens to provide a contrast with the natural landscape beyond, and Tudor gardens were, therefore, dominated by formal designs and geometric arrangements, variously described as knots, parterres, labyrinths and mazes, with short, clipped hedges, beds of flowers, gravels or coloured earths combining to give the appearance of embroidery on the ground. Such gardens were of course immensely expensive and labour-intensive to construct and maintain; they also required raised platforms and mounts if they were to be seen to the best advantage. Topiary work also became popular during the early sixteenth century, and John Leland in *c*.1520 was obviously impressed by the gardens beside the Earl of Northumberland's castle at Wressle (Yorkshire). As at Thornbury and Mells there was an inner private garden and an orchard with prospect mounds or raised viewing points beyond

the [exceedingly fair] gardens within the moat, and the orchards without. And in the orchards were mounts *opere topiaris* writhen about with degrees like the turnings of cockleshells, to come to the top without pain.

Leland also commented upon the topiary work at Little Haseley (Oxfordshire) in the garden beside the medieval manor house of Sir William Barantyne, with 'marvellous fair walks *topiarii operis*, and orchards and pools'. Like Mells, the garden at Wressle also had mounts or prospect mounds, giving views over the park and across the surrounding countryside. Many of these ideas derived from the royal gardens at Richmond and Hampton Court, both of which were designed, regardless of expense, to add magnificence and splendour to the royal palaces and to provide walks, secret arbours, displays of heraldry, regal symbols, pools of water, fountains and views.[4]

Only the wealthiest in the land could afford gardens of such magnifence. Lord Burghley, who built the palace at Theobalds (Hertfordshire) between 1564 and 1585 and laid out the elaborate pleasure garden, over 3ha (7 acres) in extent, confessed that he had a weakness for gardening and spent too much on it. He 'greatlie delighted in making gardens, fountaines and walkes.' The house cost at least £12,000 and a similar amount was spent on the garden which was supervised by the famous herbalist, John Gerard, whose *Herball*, published in 1597, was dedicated to Lord Burghley. The Great Garden at Theobalds was surrounded by a wall, and was divided into nine sections, each edged with box and arranged with trees, flowers, grass borders, fountains, statues, obelisks and stretches of water.[5]

## Sport and recreation

As well as gardens and orchards, sixteenth-century estate-owners, with their new-found wealth and new ideas of status and their proper place in society, wished to provide for leisure, sport and recreation. Thus the royal gardens at Richmond during the early sixteenth century had 'houses of pleasure to disport in' with facilities for chess, cards, dice, bowls, tennis and archery. In the same way the Long Galleries which became such a fashionable feature of the 'new' architecture provided a space for exercise and games as well as for the exhibition of paintings and portraits, and several houses at the end of the century also incorporated indoor riding schools, where horses could be exercised during periods of bad weather. Examples of these survive at Wolfeton House (Dorset), Welbeck Abbey (Nottinghamshire), Corsham (Wiltshire), Hinton St George (Somerset) and Bolsover Castle (Derbyshire), the last designed for the Duke of Newcastle by Robert Smythson. Both archery and bowls were extremely popular, and the gardens of many great houses included archery butts and a bowling green. For example, Sir Christopher Hatton's mansion at Holdenby (Northamptonshire) had an elaborate pleasure garden, of which the earthworks survive and include a pond, walks, flower-beds, lawns, a summer bower, banqueting house and a bowling green.[6]

During the early seventeenth century Anthony Ashley Cooper, the first Earl of Shaftesbury, described how the bowling green at Sixpenny Handley (Dorset) was frequented by all the leading landowners of the neighbourhood. At Pishiobury (Hertfordshire) the Elizabethan courtier, Sir Walter Mildmay, equipped his house with 'a fair Bowling Green, raised about 5 foot high, enclosed with a brick wall topped with stone, and balls upon it'. Buckhurst House (Sussex) possessed a Tudor tennis court, 20m (65ft) long, designed for the game of real tennis. During the later sixteenth century Sir Thomas Tresham laid out a garden and bowling green at Rushton (in addition to building the famous triangular Warrener's Lodge) and thousands of tons of earth were moved in order to level the ground.[7] The fact that gardens were now intended purely for pleasure, and that herbs, vegetables and fruit were relegated to separate plots or outer areas, is also illustrated by the growing popularity during the sixteenth century of prospect mounds within gardens, of bowers or summer houses and of banqueting houses.

The royal garden at Hampton Court had a large mound or mount in *c.*1530, giving views across the Thames, and later in the century Lord Burghley's garden at Theobalds had a mount with a labyrinth or maze. The garden of New College, Oxford has a fine artificial mound, begun in 1594, which gives a view over the town walls, and there was a similar prospect mount in the gardens of Wadham College. In Sir Francis Bacon's essay *Of Gardens* published in 1625 he recommends mounts at the boundary of a garden from which 'to look abroad into the fields' and also suggests a high mound in the centre of the garden surmounted by a banqueting house. Banqueting houses in which spiced delicacies, wine, fruit or cakes were served became extremely popular during the sixteenth century and after. Sir William Sharrington included two small rooms for banquets in the octagonal tower which he added to the former nunnery buildings at Lacock (Wiltshire) in *c.*1550, and Sir John Thynne had several such small rooms built on the roof at Longleat during the 1560s. Few major Elizabethan gardens were without a banqueting house and some were large buildings, like Sir Christopher Hatton's three-storey banqueting house at Holdenby (Northamptonshire) or the ornate structure built by the Vavasour family in their garden at Weston Hall (Yorkshire).

The sixteenth century also saw the development of a craze for lodges or small houses built some distance away from the main mansion to which the estate owner might retire either with his friends or for solitude and privacy. One of the best known is Sir Thomas Tresham's Triangular Lodge at Rushton (Northamptonshire), built in honour of the Trinity and as an outspoken declaration of Tresham's attachment to the Catholic faith in spite of all the persecution it brought him. Both in its construction and its decoration the lodge is full of symbolism, all centred on the figure 3, and all proclaiming its builder's steadfast belief. Sir Thomas Tresham also began, but never completed, a much larger lodge or isolated house on his estate in Northamptonshire, known as Lyveden New Bield, which was planned to contain a kitchen, dining room, drawing room and bedrooms. He also designed an elaborate garden to surround his lodge at Lyveden, with a moat, fishponds, wooded walks, arbours, terraces, orchards, rose gardens, strawberry beds and prospect mounds.

On his estate at Sherborne Castle (Dorset) Sir Walter Ralegh built a lodge with four towers as a retreat to which he might retire for solitude; while at Wothorpe (Northamptonshire), near Sir William Cecil's great house at Burghley, the lodge built by Lord Exeter early in the seventeenth century was said to be for his lordship 'to retire to out of the dust while his great house was a-sweeping'. When the scholars who were ordered by King James I to produce the Authorized Version of the Bible in the early seventeenth century translated Isaiah's description of the lonely and abandoned Daughter of Zion as being 'like a lodge in a garden of cucumbers', they could be confident that their readers would readily understand the simile.

## Eviction of tenants

From the late fifteenth century the owners of estates began to have another effect upon the landscape which is still very apparent in many parts of the English countryside. This was the forcible depopulation of numerous hamlets and villages, and the eviction of tenants. There were two reasons for this. The first was the growing desire for privacy, and the ideal of the house within its own walled park to which access could be carefully regulated. The creation of such isolated houses, situated in solitary splendour, surrounded by carefully landscaped grounds and excluding all undesirable influences continued and gathered pace during the seventeenth and eighteenth centuries, but began in the sixteenth century.

The second motive for the eviction of tenants and the removal of villages was to turn land over to profitable sheep farming, abandoning the labour-intensive business of arable cultivation and corn growing as part of a mixed-farming economy which had traditionally supported most English rural communities. Many of the affected settlements, however, were on marginal land and were already undergoing a slow decline long before their final destruction.[8]

Early examples of the removal of villages or hamlets in order to secure solitude for estate owners occurred with the foundation of some monastic houses. When a community of Cistercian monks settled in Ryedale (Yorkshire) in 1143 they removed the village of Byland to a new position over a mile away in order to obtain the peace and seclusion they desired. The small village of Pipewell (Northamptonshire) was destroyed to make room for a Cistercian abbey in 1163. Likewise, when the first Carthusian house in England was founded at Witham (Somerset) by Henry II as part of his penance for the murder of Archbishop Becket in 1170, the inhabitants of that remote part of the forest of Selwood were removed and provided with lands in another, distant part of the county. Another early example occurred at Pendley near Tring (Hertfordshire) during the mid-fifteenth century. Sir Robert Whittingham was granted the right to make a park there in

1440, and the creation of his new park excluded his tenants from their former grazing lands so that they were obliged to leave. Many years later witnesses recalled that Pendley had been a populous settlement and that

there were in the town above thirteen plows besides divers handecraft men, as tailors, shoemakers and cardmakers with divers others. The town was after-wards cast down and laid to pasture by Sir Robert Whittingham.

At Great Sandon (Staffordshire) the Erdeswicke family pulled down the village during the sixteenth century and enlarged their parkland to include the site. Only the parish church was left, isolated within the park, like so many other English parish churches whose situation emphasizes the power of the gentry families and the continuing close association between these ruling dynasties and the Church of England.

Most estate owners did not seek to put a barrier of distance between themselves and their tenants during the later Middle Ages, and at many monasteries large and busy communities rapidly grew up on the edge of the monastic precinct. But during the sixteenth century the attitude of estate owners began to change. The building of Nonsuch Palace (Surrey) which was begun by Henry VIII in 1538 and on which the King spent more than £23,000 during the next seven years, involved the removal of the village of Cuddington and its church to make room for the vast building, together with two large parks, one of which, Worcester Park, was 364ha (900 acres) in extent. The Tudor historian and topographer William Camden was so impressed by Nonsuch Palace that he described it as 'built with so much splendour and elegance that . . . you would think the whole science of architecture exhausted on this building'. During the 1580s the creation of a formal garden around the huge house built by Sir Christopher Hatton at Holdenby

Hall (Northamptonshire) led to the removal of the cottages from part of Holdenby village and these were rebuilt around a green at the other end of the village, further from the great house, although the village remained as a landscape feature which could be viewed from the house, and the church was incorporated into the garden.[9]

At Stalbridge (Dorset) during the early years of the seventeenth century the Earl of Castlehaven built a large mansion near the small town. After much difficulty and controversy he persuaded or cajoled his tenants into giving up their rights of common in return for money payments so that he might enclose his house and the whole surrounding area within a great wall more than 2m (6 feet) high and 8km (5 miles) in length. This still survives as a monument to aristocratic power and a reminder of R.H. Tawney's bitter remark on such parks, made

for those motives of social amenity and osten-tation which have done so much to make the English countryside the admiration of travellers, and so much to ruin the English peasantry.

The Earl was a notorious profligate, and in 1631 he was tried and executed for a series of bestial crimes including rape and sodomy. The house passed to his relative Richard Boyle, first Earl of Cork, who employed the famous French gardener, designer and hydraulic engineer, Saloman de Caus, to lay out a pleasure garden at Stalbridge. The house and grounds were inherited by the Earl's younger son, Robert Boyle, the mathematician and scientist, who spent his boyhood there.[10]

In Cambridgeshire Sir John Cutts removed the small village of Childerley in order to lay out a deer park and garden around his house, and today only the hollow-ways of the former village streets and the grass-covered mounds of the house sites survive as evidence of the removal. Sir Robert Cotton, the eminent antiquary, whose collection of manuscripts is now in the British Library, evicted some of his tenants at Conington (Huntingdonshire) during the early years of the seventeenth century, partly in order to lay the land to grass for sheep farming and partly because their houses abutted the terrace and garden which was laid out as part of the grounds of the mansion he was building there. Only the large late-medieval church survives as evidence of the former prosperity of the parishioners, and this is now filled with the monuments and memorials of the Cotton family.[11] At the vast mansion which he built at such expense at Hatfield (Hertfordshire) during the early years of the seventeenth century, Robert Cecil, Lord Salisbury, was able totally to rearrange the landscape and paid some of his own copyhold tenants to leave their lands so that he could extend his park and ensure his own seclusion.

Many other newly-rich families were also able to build new mansions standing within their own grounds and isolated from any neighbouring settlements. These new mansions were generally in elevated situations, outward-looking towards the distant views, with large windows and tall, elaborate frontages dominating the surrounding countryside, very different from the enclosed courtyard or cloistered houses of previous generations. Examples which show the influence of Renaissance ideas and the desire for a new standard of symmetry and Classical forms include Longleat (Wiltshire), on the site of a former Augustinian house and secluded within its great park, Burton Agnes Hall (Yorkshire) designed like Longleat by Robert Smythson, or another Smythson house, Wollaton Hall (Nottinghamshire), built for Sir Francis Willoughby as a showpiece in a commanding situation and surrounded by its park, or Compton Wynates (Warwickshire), and Hengrave Hall (Suffolk) built for the London merchant, Sir Thomas Kytson.

The wholesale removal of settlements and the ruthless destruction of ancient villages in order to enlarge a park or create an unobstructed view were to become much more common in the eighteenth century – most sixteenth-century evictions of tenants and destruction of their cottages by estate owners served a quite different purpose. Their object was to increase the revenue of the estate by turning the land from arable to pasture. A slackening demand for corn and a continuing ready market for wool meant that large-scale sheep farming became increasingly profitable during the later fifteenth century and throughout the early decades of the sixteenth century. Estate owners were, therefore, eager to increase their sheep flocks or to let their land to the masters of large flocks who could pay much higher rents than traditional small-scale arable farmers. Examples of former estate villages and hamlets deserted for this reason are to be found throughout the country. In Warwickshire landowners such as the Lucys, Catesbys and Spencers built up huge flocks of sheep during the late fifteenth century, and as a result at least 120 settlements in the county were depopulated and abandoned.[12]

One of the best-known examples of such eviction in Warwickshire occurred at Wormleighton where the Spencer family evicted their tenants in *c.* 1500 and converted the land to pasture. In place of the former tenants many thousands of sheep were kept and the wool sold to wholesalers in London and Norwich. At Wormleighton the earthworks of the village are clearly visible in the landscape, and are a potent reminder of aristocratic power; only the medieval church and the manor house of the Spencers, together with estate houses, survive from the once-prosperous medieval settlement. Similar evictions occurred in many parts of the country. They are reflected in the many surviving earthworks of the former villages, hamlets and farmsteads and in the desperate but generally ineffectual protests which the tenants addressed to the courts. One way of getting the tenants to leave was by greatly increasing the rents and fines for entry upon their tenements and holdings. In 1600 the former tenants of the village of Heene (Kent) complained that their landlords

for their own private gain and lucre, in the six years past have taken the said houses (which numbered 60) into their own hands, turned out the inhabitants by great fines . . . the orchards are dug up, the town is depopulated and there remains no sign of the houses.[13]

To the south of Dorchester (Dorset) there is a string of deserted settlements along the shallow valley of the south Winterborne as it runs around the Iron Age hillfort of Maiden Castle. The tenants were evicted from these settlements during the sixteenth century so that the lands could be converted to pasture and used for large-scale sheep farming. The records of the bitter complaints made by the tenants show the pressures they faced as more and more sheep were kept by the landlords. At Winterborne Ashton the tenants were forced to leave in c.1500 because of the sheep flocks kept by the Newburgh family who owned the land there. In 1521 the tenants of Winterborne Came complained that their landlord, Sir William Filliol, was so overstocking their pastures with his sheep and converting ancient arable to grassland that 'because of the greate oppressions and injuries' they would not be able to pay their rent 'nor Able to Abide in their countrey by cause of the said greate oppressions'. Similar complaints came from the other settlements along the valley, but obviously these pleas failed, for Winterborne Herringston, Ashton, Farringdon, Came and Whitcombe are all deserted. At Winterborne Farringdon a fragment of wall from the former parish church survives amid the clearly-defined earthworks of the former village. The church still existed in 1630 when a local author Thomas Gerard described the site as

a lone church, for there is hardlie any house left in the parish, such of late hath been the Covetousness of some private Men, that to increase their Demesnes have depopulated whole parishes.

During the early sixteenth century all these settlements along the Winterborne valley had supported numerous households, but by the time of the Hearth Tax in 1662 Winterborne Herringston had only three remaining households, Winterborne Came had only two and Winterborne Farringdon was completely deserted.[14]

## Extension of parks

As the desire for isolation and privacy increased among the gentry more and more houses were built within parks, or parks were extended to include houses. At the same time many of the older hunting parks fell out of use or became useless as deer reserves because the expensive but necessary maintenance work was not kept up. Many of the former monastic deer parks were converted to more profitable agricultural uses by their new owners, for example on Cranborne Chase the former park at Blagdon was ploughed up and used for the cultivation of woad, a demanding but highly-profitable plant used as the basis of all dark-coloured dyes in the cloth industry.[15] Writing of Cornwall in 1602 Richard Carew commented that many deer parks had disappeared and that the owners were 'making theire deere leape over the pale to give bullocks place'.[16]

The royal forests and parks were also subject to continual encroachment during the sixteenth century. In the New Forest the fattening of pigs became an important industry and Thomas Fuller later described how the pigs 'feed in the forest on plenty of acorns . . . which going out lean, return home fat, without care or cost to their owners'.[17] In the royal forests of Wiltshire local landowners used every excuse to encroach upon the royal lands. Sir Henry Baynton enclosed Spye Park out of the royal forest of Pewsham, and was said to have killed the royal deer, felled the trees and built cottages for his tenants in the forest. Both Baynton and the royal keepers were said to have 'mayntayned their whole houses and families on venison, and made it theire ordinarie Meate, and gave their servants noe other foode'. Likewise in Selwood forest, Sir John Thynne carved his park at Longleat from the surrounding woodland, and the Duke of Somerset created a park at Savernake, in spite of the protests of his tenants, who had traditionally enjoyed rights of pasture and other privileges in the forest. In Hertfordshire much of Waltham forest and of the parklands around Theobalds, on which both William Cecil and James I had spent such vast sums of money, were once more converted to agriculture. In 1613 the poet, Michael Drayton, commented on the progression in land use over the centuries from ploughland to forest or deer park and back again to arable once more

> The Ridge and Furrow shewes, that once the
>     crooked Plow,
> Turned up the grassy turfe, where Okes are
>     rooted now:
> And at this houre we see, the Share and
>     Coulter teare
> The full corne-bearing gleabe, where
>     sometimes forests were.

The final disafforestation of the royal forests during the reign of Charles I, a process hastened by the penury of the royal treasury, proved to be very unpopular with the tenants who possessed common rights in the forest. Although they were allocated other lands in lieu of their rights, they felt cheated by the changes, and during the 1630s there were numerous riots protesting against disafforestation. Some of the most violent were in the south-west, where the rioters were given an imaginary unity by the fictitious figure of 'Lady Skimmington', who was supposed to be their leader and champion. At Gillingham (Dorset) the rioters refused to disperse and successfully defied the royal troops with the words 'Here were we born and here we stay'. Eventually the riots were suppressed, but they constituted the largest single popular uprising against royal policy until the outbreak of the Civil War. The protests against disafforestation are ironic in view of the bitter hatred which had been aroused by the imposition and extension of the royal forests during the Middle Ages.[18]

## Suppression of the monasteries

The most important feature which influenced the growth of estates and the increasing wealth and power of the great landowners during the sixteenth century was the dissolution of the monastic houses under Henry VIII and the suppression of the chantries during the reign of Edward VI. The confiscation by the Crown of all the lands and property of these religious institutions brought unprecedented quantities of land on to the market and led to an intense scramble among the aristocracy, gentry and wealthy merchants to secure former monastic sites, buildings and lands (Fig. 15). For many of those with the available wealth and the necessary good fortune to profit from this massive dispersal of lands, their purchases were to form the foundation of the subsequent fortunes of their families. All over the country the timely acquisition of monastic spoils led to the rapid rise of a host of new families, drawn from the ranks of royal servants and courtiers, royal officials, lawyers, local administrators, former monastic stewards, speculators and newly-rich merchants.

**15** *Lacock Abbey (Wiltshire). Founded as a house of Augustinian canonesses in c.1230, the nunnery church stood in the foreground of this illustration. The church was demolished by Sir William Sharington, who acquired the property at the Dissolution; he turned the cloisters into a mansion for himself, and built the tower as a banqueting house.*

The speed with which the monastic lands were dispersed by the Crown can be seen in Hertfordshire where of 168 manors which were in royal possession in 1540 all but 12 had been disposed of by 1550.[19] In the south-east of England more than two-thirds of the land had been alienated by the end of Henry VIII's reign in 1547, while in Somerset the Crown had sold 63 per cent of the former monastic lands by 1558, and by the early 1570s as much as 85 per cent of the lands and property had been purchased by private individuals.[20] In Kent during the sixteenth century the gentry increased their landholding by more than a third.

Even the most conservative and those who remained most firmly attached to the Catholic faith did not scruple to purchase former monastic lands, and by the early seventeenth century there were few leading families whose fortunes and estates had not been augmented by the spoil of the religious houses. The effect on the landscape was enormous. Monastic churches, cloisters and domestic buildings were rapidly demolished by the new owners in order either to sell the lead from the roofs to recoup some of the purchase money, or to use the stone, timber and tiles for other purposes. Many magnificent buildings and entire monastic houses were totally demolished. Thus of 69 former religious houses in Sussex, 41 have

almost completely disappeared. The scale of
the destruction and the quality of the
buildings which were destroyed is still
apparent from the ruins which survive,
especially in the remains of the great
Cistercian abbeys of the north of England.
At Roche Abbey, for example, the choir
stalls were burned to melt the lead from the
roofs, while the building was demolished
and the stone sold. An observer described
how

All things of price [were] either spoiled, carped
away, or defaced to the uttermost . . . it seemeth
that every person bent himself to filch and spoil
what he could . . . nothing was spared . . .[21]

In 1540 the nunnery of Amesbury
(Wiltshire) was acquired by Sir Edward
Seymour, later Duke of Somerset, and soon
afterwards the buildings were systematically
destroyed for the sake of the lead;
gunpowder was used to bring down the
spire of the nuns' church so that the lead
could easily be removed, and within a short
time all the buildings were in ruins. The lead
was melted down on the site and was sold
together with stone, timber, paving slabs,
gravestones, glass, doors and windows.[22] At
former monastic houses all over the country
the same process was taking place.

During the reign of Edward VI the
chantry foundations, together with
numerous schools, hospitals and
almshouses, were also suppressed and their
lands and property sold. For those with the
necessary wealth and business acumen, the
sixteenth century offered opportunities for
huge profits and increases in landholdings,
with unprecedented sales of Crown lands at
a time of rapidly increasing land values and
a great rise in the prices which could be
obtained for agricultural produce. The
combined effect on the landscape was
apparent everywhere. In a few places the
monastic churches were purchased by
parishioners and survived as parish
churches, for example at Bolton, Selby and

**16**   *The gatehouse of the Benedictine Abbey of Cerne
Abbas (Dorset). This fine building is one of the few
remaining fragments of the monastic buildings of this
abbey. It escaped destruction at the Dissolution by
being turned into a dwelling.*

Malton (Yorkshire), Romsey and
Christchurch (Hampshire), or Sherborne
(Dorset). Much more common was the
conversion of the monastic buildings into
residences for their new owners (Fig. 16). In
some cases the existing buildings were
converted, as at Mottisfont (Hampshire),
Combe Abbey (Warwickshire), Milton
Abbas (Dorset), Buckland Abbey (Devon)
and many others; elsewhere the monastic
buildings were demolished to be replaced by
new country houses such as Calke Abbey

(Derbyshire), Langley Priory (Leicestershire), Fountains Hall (Yorkshire) or Longleat and Wilton (Wiltshire).

It was largely wealth derived from their profitable dealings in former monastic lands that financed the building of so many of the great houses of Elizabethan and early Stuart England. In Staffordshire, James Leveson of Wolverhampton, who had made a fortune from dealing in wool, was able to purchase the lands and buildings of the Augustinian house at Trentham, as well as a large estate in neighbouring Shropshire which had belonged to Lilleshall Abbey. His purchases elevated the family to the status of landed gentry, and during the 1630s they built a large mansion on the site of the former priory at Trentham. During the early seventeenth century the Robartes family of Truro, who had made a huge fortune from tin mining, were able to purchase the former monastic land at Lanhydrock and build there a grand Jacobean mansion, and yet still

retain sufficient wealth to purchase a peerage for £10,000 in 1625. Likewise, the Sneyd family purchased the monastic lands at Keele, and during the reign of Elizabeth, Ralph Sneyd built a fine house on a prominent position away from the village and from the ruins of the former religious house and isolated within its own park.[23]

Houses which were designed to provide a conspicuous display of wealth and a public statement of political and social status included Wollaton (Nottinghamshire), Hardwick Hall (Derbyshire), Longleat (Wiltshire), Welbeck Abbey (Nottinghamshire) and Basing House (Hampshire). The last was a huge mansion built by Sir William Paulet, first Marquess of Winchester, who, in spite of his Catholic faith, acquired a vast estate based on former monastic land, and openly stated that he took the willow and not the oak for his emblem and bent to the prevailing wind.[24]

# 4 Fashions and design in landscape development during the seventeenth century

Interest in the development of their houses and country estates, enthusiasm for the latest fashions in architecture, parks, gardens and estate management, and an increasing appreciation of their estates as a reflection of wealth, power and status, continued to grow among all sections of the aristocracy and gentry during the seventeenth century. A lead was taken by the royal family with the development by James I and Charles I of the gardens and landscape of Somerset House, Richmond, Greenwich, Wimbledon and other royal residences.[1] Likewise, many of the richest and most influential families built extravagant palaces or 'prodigy' houses, many of them far larger than could ever be required for living in, and often outstripping in cost even the prodigious wealth of their builders. Some were built in order to accommodate Queen Elizabeth or James I and their enormous retinues during their occasional 'progresses' through their kingdom; others simply as an ostentatious display of wealth or in order to surpass the houses of rivals.

The profitable posts, offices, sinecures and other favours which royal patronage could bestow, ensured that there was no lack of courtiers and politicians anxious to impress successive monarchs with their lavish hospitality. The Lord Chancellor, Sir Christopher Hatton, built an enormous palace at Holdenby (Northamptonshire), in its size and splendour one of the marvels of the Elizabethan age; the Cecil family built or renewed Theobalds (Hertfordshire), Hatfield (Hertfordshire) and Cranborne (Dorset); the Howards created Audley End (Essex), the Sackvilles erected Knole (Kent), the Thynnes built the huge house at Longleat (Wiltshire), and Sir Edward Phelips, the Master of the Rolls under Queen Elizabeth, completed Montacute (Somerset) before the end of the Queen's reign.

In Derbyshire the vast pile of Hardwick Hall was built by the formidable Elizabeth, countess of Shrewsbury, known as 'Bess of Hardwick', who used the vast income which she had acquired through her marriages to finance the transformation of nearly a dozen houses, including the new mansion at Chatsworth. In Nottinghamshire, Wollaton Hall was built for Sir Francis Willoughby at a cost of more than £8000, and in addition large sums were spent on laying out the grounds with formal gardens, walks, plantations together with carefully contrived vistas.

Further north, two examples from Yorkshire are Fountains Hall, which was built using stone from the former Cistercian abbey by the successful merchant and entrepreneur, Sir Stephen Proctor, and Burton Agnes designed by the Elizabethan architect, Robert Smythson, for Sir Henry Griffith and built during the early years of James I's reign.

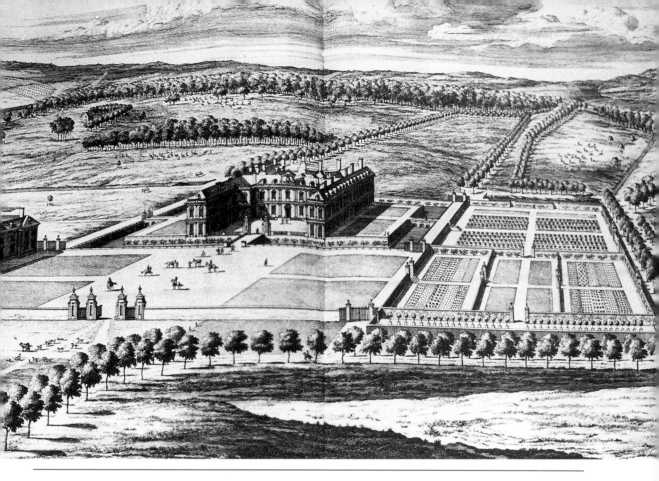

17  *Althorp Park (Northamptonshire). Mansion, gardens avenues and woodlands at Althorp Park, the centre of the Spencer estates. From Kip and Knyff,* Britannia Illustrata, *1709.*

## The house in the landscape

Throughout the country the seventeenth century witnessed the creation of innumerable parks, gardens, woodland walks, lakes, fountains and other landscape features. There was a fascination with formal garden design and a growing interest in garden features such as temples, grottoes, statues and obelisks, and with curiosities such as mobile sculptures, automata, elaborate fountains and other devices worked by water pressure. A new concern developed for views from the house, both across the pleasure garden and over the landscape beyond. Parks and parkland were no longer regarded as something separate from the house, and throughout the Stuart period new houses were being built set in solitary splendour within carefully contrived landscapes, with park walls, entrance lodges, plantations, lakes and pavilions, all intended to give dignity and distinction to the house and to emphasize the gulf between the owner and his social inferiors beyond the park pales (Fig. 17). For example, when the wealthy London merchant and industrialist, Sir Arthur Ingram, acquired the medieval castle and estate at Sheriff Hutton (Yorkshire) during the reign of James I, he abandoned the castle and built a new mansion isolated within its own park. Likewise, the Brudenell family greatly enlarged their park at Deene (Northamptonshire) during the early seventeenth century to create a fitting setting for their Tudor mansion, stocking the park with large numbers of red and fallow deer.[2] The Bampfield family of Hardington near Frome (Somerset) depopulated the village leaving only their own mansion, stables and farm, together with the medieval parish church. On the former village fields they laid out a large park with formal gardens, a deer enclosure, rabbit warren and a gazebo from which to survey the whole area.

As early as 1583 it was reported that the village had been destroyed and only 'Mr Bamfielde's house' remained

the which village is wholly enclosed and made pasture; and no house lefte but his owne, and he pulleth downe the churche, and it is scarse knowne where the parsonage house stode . . .

In fact the church survived and the interior is now dominated by a large monument of 1694 to Colonel Warwick Bampfield.[3]

On her journeys through England at the end of the seventeenth century Celia Fiennes approvingly notes numerous houses which had been built to give a view across the surrounding countryside. For example, at Stoke Edith (Herefordshire) the new house which had been built by the Foley family from the profits of their ironworks was on a hill overlooking the estate 'and gives a greate view of the country which most belongs to Mr Foley'. She describes the gravel walks, terraces and long straight avenues of trees, and the 'vast prospect of the country, it being situated on the ascent of a hill'. At her relative Sir Griffith Boynton's house at Burton Agnes (Yorkshire), she delighted in the fact that from the windows of the upper gallery of the house there was a vast prospect 'out of which you view the whole Country round, and discover the shipps under saile though att a good distance'.[4] During her journey through Derbyshire in 1697, Celia Fiennes was enchanted by the gardens of Chatsworth, and especially by the ingenious waterworks and fountains, and she described at length

. . . severall fine Gardens one without another with gravell walkes and squairs of grass with stone statues in them, and in the middle of each Garden is a large fountaine full of images of Sea Gods and Dolphins and Sea Horses which are full of pipes which spout out water in the bason and spouts all about the gardens.[4]

Enthusiasm for gardens and garden design became, as it was to remain, a national obsession, and prodigious sums were spent upon parks, park walls, gardens and their maintenance. Lord Burghley's son, Sir Robert Cecil, inherited his father's love of gardens and lavished enormous sums of money on Hatfield House (Hertfordshire), totally re-ordering and changing the surrounding landscape. His proceedings illustrate both the wealth available to such a major political figure and royal servant, and also the legal limitations on his power, for he was obliged to purchase from his own tenants their rights in the arable lands which lay close to his house, paying them as much as £10 per acre and providing them with land elsewhere. He could then achieve the seclusion and separation from inferiors he sought, and lay out the landscape to provide an appropriate setting for his mansion.

Cecil's gardens at Hatfield included terraces, raised walks, waterworks and a fountain, while gifts of fruit trees, vines and other plants came from those who sought his favours. To maintain his garden a large number of gardeners and labourers was employed, while John Tradescant the Elder, who was later to achieve great fame for his work in introducing new plants from the Continent, was commissioned to import fruit trees, seeds and plants by the shipload from Holland and France.[5]

At the same time that he was spending so much on Hatfield, Robert Cecil was also rebuilding the former royal hunting lodge at Cranborne (Dorset) where he entertained the king. His work there included gatehouses, lodges, terraces and a formal, walled garden made up of nine rectangular beds with a mount or prospect mound giving views over the landscape beyond. Sadly, Cecil died in 1612 before his work at Hatfield and Cranborne was complete.

Robert Cecil's cousin, Francis Bacon, undertook enormous building and landscape work at Gorhambury (Hertfordshire) including the creation of a notable formal garden and an elaborate water garden which covered some 4 acres and included a banqueting house on an island and a viewing mount from which the whole garden could be admired. Francis Bacon published his ideas of appropriate garden design in his essay 'Of Gardens' in 1625 with its striking opening

God Almightie first planted a Garden. And indeed it is the Purest of Human pleasures. It is the Greatest Refreshment to the Spirits of Man; without which Buildings and Pallaces are but Grosse Handy-Workes . . .

Francis Bacon died in 1626, but thirty years later the seventeenth-century antiquary John Aubrey visited the garden and was greatly impressed by what he saw. He described the long straight avenues of trees, the oak wood with its fine shady trees, under-planted with flowers such as paeonies and tulips, the

**18**   *Longleat (Wiltshire). The formal gardens which were later to be swept away by Capability Brown. From Kip and Knyff,* Britannia Illustrata, *1709.*

plantations of cherry, plum and other fruit trees, the formal walks with viewing points with elegant summer houses, and the ponds whose bottoms were lined with carefully-selected coloured pebbles.

In the middle of the middlemost pond, in the Island, is a curious banquetting house of Roman architecture, paved with black and white marble; covered with Cornish slatt, and neatly wainscotted.[6]

Slightly earlier, Sir John Oglander, whose estate was at Nunwell on the Isle of Wight, became an expert on the cultivation of fruit trees. In his journal he recorded that he planted with his own hands at Nunwell

. . . a hundred Portugal quinces, Pippins, pearmains, puttes, hornies, and other good apples, and all sorts of pears . . . cherries,

damsons, and plums. In the upper gardens, apricocks, mellecatoons, and figs. In the Court, vines and apricocks; in the Bowling Green the vine and infinity of raspberries . . . When my successors hereafter reap the fruits of my labours, let them remember the founder.

Amidst all his political activities and court intrigues Anthony Ashley Cooper, first Earl of Shaftesbury, also found time to take an active interest in his garden at Wimborne St Giles (Dorset). Among his papers is a *Book of Memorandums* written during the 1670s, in which he made copious notes about plants, fruit trees, roses and other flowers. He noted the qualities of the different fruits and refers to trees and plants to be obtained from London, France and elsewhere, as well as from the estates of friends and neighbours. Among the entries are long lists of different

**19**  *Westbury Court garden, Westbury-on-Severn (Gloucestershire). Created by Maynard Colchester c.1700, this is the best surviving example of the sort of formal water garden which became so popular during the later seventeenth century.*

sorts of plums, peaches, nectarines, cherries, pears, apples and grapes, as well as turnips, carrots, parsnips, potatoes, liquorice, mustard seed, caraway seed, physic herbs etc., noting the best varieties, season of use, sources of supply and instructions to the gardener. The Earl's notes also contain recipes, although his taste seems somewhat suspect for he suggested that

A gallon of Elder Berrys to a hogshead of cider or perry makes excellent clarett, press them with the apples or peares.[7]

## Geometry in the garden

Most seventeenth-century garden designs were rigidly formal and geometric, with the straight lines of elaborately arranged borders rectangular 'canals' of water, a great deal of closely-clipped shrubs, and topiary work or box hedging. Even vast gardens such as Chatsworth or Castle Howard were laid out in this fashion. Later in the seventeenth century the inspiration for such formality and the imposition of uniformity and symmetry upon an ordered landscape came from the French court and especially from the great garden at Versailles laid out to emphasize the grandeur of 'Le Roi Soleil', Louis XIV, by his famous gardener, André Le Nôtre.

Most of these English formal gardens were swept away during the eighteenth century in obedience to new ideas of taste and style, but a few survivors or restorations remain to give an idea of the formal elegance of these labour-intensive creations. There is a reconstructed knot garden at Hampton Court and in the Queen's Garden at Kew. Chastleton House (Oxfordshire) is the early seventeenth-century house built by Walter Jones, a Witney wool merchant who purchased the estate from Robert Catesby, one of the Gunpowder Plot conspirators. It has been little altered and although the formal garden

**20** *Westbury Court garden, Westbury-on-Severn. Pavilion overlooking the formal garden and straight canal.*

was replanted in the nineteenth century it preserves the form of the original. This consisted of a round enclosure with a sun-dial at its centre, and concentric circles of rose-beds, box shrubs closely clipped into fantastic topiary work in the shape of beasts, a circular yew-hedge, with an outer circle of flower beds. 'At Chastleton we are as near as we can get to a surviving geometrical Mannerist garden from the Jacobean age.'[8]

A seventeenth-century garden also survives at Ashdown House near Lambourn on the high Berkshire downland. The house was built by the Earl of Craven for

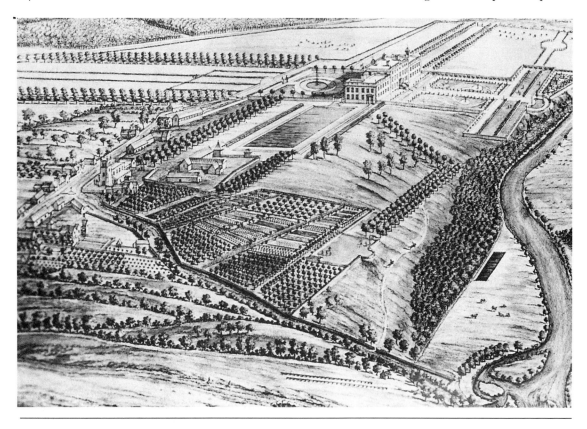

**21**   *Sprotbrough Hall (Yorkshire). From Kip and Knyff* Britannia Illustrata, *1709. The hall was demolished in 1926.*

Elizabeth, Queen of Bohemia in *c*.1660, and is constructed of chalk blocks with stone dressings; the geometric garden was laid out at the same time, with a box-hedged parterre flanked by avenues of trees. The formal garden of *c*.1770 survives at Levens Hall (Westmorland) and is notable for its remarkable collection of topiary work. Another interesting survivor is the late seventeenth-century water garden at Westbury Court (Gloucestershire) (Fig. 19). The house has been demolished but the formal garden which was laid out between 1698 and 1705 remains. It consists of two straight 'canals' or geometrically arranged lakes in parallel, with a two-storey red brick pavilion (Fig. 20) at one end, raised on white columns, giving a view over the whole garden. At the other end of the garden are

wrought-iron clairvoyées or open-work gates through which a vista can be obtained across the surrounding countryside of the Severn valley and to the Forest of Dean beyond.

Other houses where the formality and symmetry of seventeenth-century gardens can be appreciated include Blickling Hall (Norfolk) where the early seventeenth-century garden has been painstakingly restored by the National Trust, Canons Ashby (Northamptonshire), St Paul's, Walden Bury (Hertfordshire), Belton (Lincolnshire) or Bramham Park (Yorkshire) which retains the long straight avenues of closely-clipped hedges and the waterworks, temples, obelisks and eye-catchers.

A remarkable source of information on

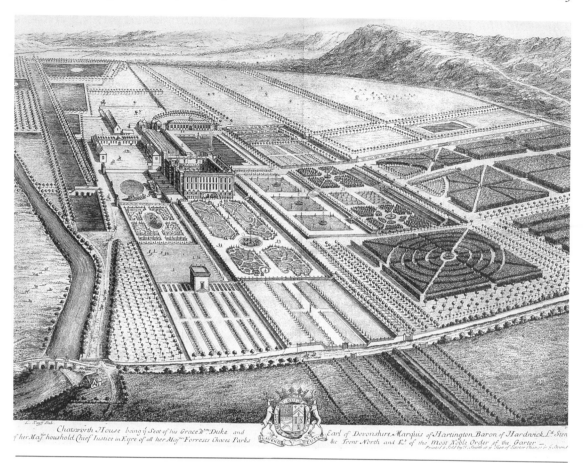

Chatsworth House being y Seat of his Grace W.m Duke     and     Earl of Devonshire, Marquis of Hartington, Baron of Hardwick L.d Sten
of her Maj.y houshold, Chief Justice in Eyre of all her Maj.ies Forrests Chaces Parks     &c Trent North and K.t of the Most Noble Order of the Garter —

**22**   *Chatsworth (Derbyshire). Mansion and formal garden, from Kip and Knyff,* Britannia Illustrata, *1709.*

the layout of seventeenth-century gardens and parks exists in the splendid engravings produced during the early years of the eighteenth century by Johannes Kip from the drawings by Leonard Knyff. These provide a bird's-eye view of numerous houses, gardens and landscapes and were published in a series of volumes beginning in 1707 under the title *Britannia Illustrata* (Figs 18, 21–3).

An example of the information provided by a Kip 'bird's-eye view' engraving is his depiction of Dunham Massey (Cheshire) in 1697. This shows the formal park and garden laid out by George Booth, Earl of Warrington (1675–1758), who, like many others before and since, sought peace and contentment, and relief from an unhappy

marriage, in building, gardening, tree-planting and the improvement of his estate. Kip's engraving shows a long avenue of trees leading from the house, the walled, ornamental garden arranged in geometric fashion with a summer house or banqueting house at one corner, and a mount or viewing point with rings of clipped hedges around it and at the summit a gazebo providing a prospect over the surrounding countryside.

In 1750 four views of the house and park were painted by John Harris, and show the result of the Earl's work. The house had been largely rebuilt, together with the stables and coach houses, the garden was rearranged, and the surrounding parkland had been transformed by a vast programme of tree-planting.

**24**  *Low Ham church (Somerset). The church was built during the mid-seventeenth century by the strongly royalist Hext and Stawell families, and stood beside their great mansion which has since been demolished.*

they had carved along the chancel screen in the church the text

> My sonne, feare God and the Kinge
> And meddle not with them that are given to
>    Change.

## Parish churches, monuments and almshouses

It was a short step from the parish church isolated in the park to the church as a virtual family chapel (Fig. 25), burial place and show case in which to display the huge memorials which it became customary to erect to members of gentry families. There are innumerable examples all over the country of parish churches whose interiors are totally overwhelmed by the number, size and opulence of the monuments which they have been obliged to accommodate. The entire chancel at Warkton (Northamptonshire) is devoted to four huge monuments to members of the Montague family; each monument is larger and more prominent than the altar (Fig. 26). Edenham church (Lincolnshire) is filled with the tombs and memorials of the Bertie family; Exton church (Rutland), now isolated within the park, is tightly packed with the monuments of the various families that have owned the property there. Belton church (Lincolnshire) is filled with the tombs of the Custs and Brownlows; at Swinbrook (Oxfordshire) the effigies of successive

**25**  *Maiden Bradley (Wiltshire). Monument in the church to Sir Edward Seymour by J.M. Rysbrack, 1728. An example of the lavish expense and superb craftsmanship of the memorials with which gentry families overloaded many English parish churches.*

members of the Fettiplace family are stacked on shelves in the chancel, each one leaning uncomfortably on one elbow. Tawstock church in north Devon stands within the grounds of Tawstock Court and is filled with the monuments of the Bourchiers and Wrays; the chancel of Lydiard Tregoze church(Wiltshire) is filled to bursting point with the huge monuments of the St John family (Fig. 27). At Ingestre (Staffordshire) the medieval church which had attracted many pilgrims to the healing shrine of

**26**  *Warkton (Northamptonshire). Monument of 1753 to Mary, Duchess of Montagu in the church.*

**27**  *Triptych in the chancel of Lydiard Tregoze church, near Swindon. The chancel is crammed with the monuments of the St John family, and this superb triptych, erected beside the altar in 1645, shows the complete genealogy of the family, with their heraldry and family connections together with a large painting of the contemporary members of the family.*

St Erasmus, was demolished by Sir Walter Chetwynd and replaced by the elegant late seventeenth-century church which is thought to have been designed by Wren. The church stands beside the fine seventeenth-century mansion, Ingestre Hall, and the interior is filled with the monuments of the Chetwynds and their successors the Talbots.

The practice of erecting sumptuous and elaborate family pews within parish churches has also greatly affected the

interiors of many churches. Lord Ashburnham's pew at Ampthill (Bedfordshire) occupied a whole gallery; it was decorated with green silk sprinkled with gold, and furnished with comfortable chairs covered in green taffeta and equipped with velvet cushions. Melton Constable church (Norfolk) is almost overwhelmed by the

**28**  *Monument, Redgrave church (Suffolk). Monument to Sir John Holt, 1710.*

**34** *Plan of Hazelbury Bryan (Dorset) 1607. Part of the widespread estates of the Earl of Northumberland, the detailed plan was drawn by Ralph Treswell, a leading cartographer of the time.*

who brought back fruit trees from London nurserymen for a new orchard at Lulworth. During 1636, for example, sums totalling £446 11s 8d were sent to London. Large-scale agricultural improvements were carried out on the estate farms, including the draining of Lodmoor on the coast near Weymouth at a cost of £40, and the former common fields at Sutton Poyntz were divided and allotted among the various tenants. Throughout the estate the tenants on each manor were strongly encouraged to co-operate in the creation of water-meadows wherever convenient chalkland streams could be used for this purpose. Thus in 1635 an agreement was made between the Duke and his tenants at Winfrith that all would share in the costs of creating a water-meadow in Winfrith Mead and that each party should contribute 'in proportion to the benefit that shall accrue to them from the improvement, to be valued by two indifferent arbitrators'. In 1636 the Duke spent a total of £116 1s 3d on surveying, trenches, sluices, hatches and other costs of laying out water-meadows at Winfrith,

Burton, Heyford and Lulworth. The early grass and abundant hay crops provided by the water-meadows meant that more sheep and cattle could be kept, and the folding of the enlarged sheep flocks on the arable lands ensured that greatly increased yields of corn could be produced.

During the same period the account books show that large sums were being spent on the grounds around the mansion at Lulworth Castle. Rabbits were purchased for restocking the warren, the fishponds were cleaned at a cost of £9 4s 8d, and a 'trammell nett' was bought for catching the fish. Each year considerable sums were spent on cutting grass and making hay for the deer and on the maintenance of the deer park. Most expensive of all was the cost of laying out the garden and creating an orchard. Clay was dug and bricks were made on the site at a cost of £111 6s 8d, while a further £210 1s 3½d was spent on the garden and on the purchase of fruit trees and shrubs for the orchard. Nathaniel Hardy was paid £1 17s 0d a year to keep the bowling green, and Amyas Burton was paid £1 10s 0d a year to catch the moles in the park and garden. Shrubs were purchased to create divisions within the formal garden and gravel was bought to lay out the paths, and glass was purchased for the windows of the summer house.

Theophilus, Duke of Suffolk died in 1641 and the Lulworth estate was sold to Humphrey Weld, a wealthy London merchant, who continued the work begun by his predecessor and completed the fantastic mock-medieval 'castle'. Successive generations of the Welds took a close personal interest in their estates, since their Catholicism debarred them from public life, and their concern is shown by the careful records and superb estate maps which they created. Although Lulworth Castle was gutted by fire in 1929, the landscaped gardens remain intact as do the garden terraces and the mellow brick walls which

the Duke of Suffolk built around his garden and orchard.[14]

## Industrial enterprise

Other gentry families sought to exploit the industrial or mineral potential of their estates. Sussex gentry families such as the Smiths, Fullers and Evelyns encouraged the iron industry of the Weald in Kent, creating in the process the hammer ponds which remain such a distinctive and attractive aspect of the landscape. Others greatly increased their fortunes through the mining of coal, such as the Dudleys or Foleys in the Black Country, the Willoughbys of Wollaton (Nottinghamshire) and the Lowthers in Cumberland. It was in order to ship coal from his mines that Sir John Lowther created the port of Whitehaven during the 1680s, on a regular grid pattern. Previously Whitehaven had been no more than a fishing village, but with the rapid expansion of the coal trade together with the export of salt and the import of tobacco, growth was dramatic and during the eighteenth century it became one of the largest and busiest ports in the country.[15] Similarly, the Curwen family promoted the growth of the port of Workington (Cumberland).

During the mid-seventeenth century, Sir John Oglander of Nunwell (Isle of Wight), claimed that it was essential for a country landowner to have some other source of income: from industry, trade or a profession.

. . . it is impossible for a mere country gentleman ever to grow rich or raise his house. He must have some other vocation with his inheritance, as to be a courtier, lawyer, merchant or some other vocation . . . By only following the plough he may keep his word and be upright, but he will never increase his fortune.[16]

Industrial enterprise was not always a sure route to wealth, however, and numerous pitfalls lay in wait for the unwary entrepreneur. A good example of this is Sir William Clavell (1568–1644) an intensely energetic landowner from Smedmore (Dorset) whose persistent attempts to exploit the natural resources of his estate all ended in failure. His estate had easy access to the sea and contained deposits of alum and copperas, both used in dyeing, as well as copious supplies of oil-bearing shale which could be burnt as fuel. Clavell's attempts to produce alum and copperas fell foul of a powerful group of courtiers to whom James I had entrusted the task of building up the alum industry as a royal enterprise. After Clavell had spent several thousand pounds on his project he was ordered to stop work by the Crown agents, and lost all his investment including the cost of a pier which he had built to ship the alum. But Clavell, 'who one Disaster dismayed not', turned to another project. This was to make glass using the oil-bearing shale as fuel, in spite of the hideous smell and thick black smoke it produces when burning. After some initial success this undertaking was also closed down by the Crown, which in 1615 had granted a monopoly of glass

**35** *Remains of a duck decoy at Nyland (Somerset). This decoy was part of the estates of the Popham family, and was one of numerous similar profitable decoys in the Somerset Levels.*

manufacture to Sir Robert Mansell, Vice-Admiral and Lord Treasurer of the Navy.

When Clavell refused to abandon his works he was imprisoned in the Marshalsea prison in 1623 and his buildings and furnaces were demolished by order of the Privy Council. After being released from prison Clavell made a final attempt to profit from the resources of his estate, and began to distil salt from sea water, using the shale as fuel. This project also failed, and Clavell was obliged to sell much of his land to pay his debts, leaving only the remnants of his pier and the wreckage of his glass furnaces as a feature in the landscape and as a memorial to the failure of his enterprises.[17]

## Duck decoys

The construction of duck decoys was an important source of profit and food which attracted the attention of many gentlemen during the seventeenth century and later, and which has left numerous traces in the landscape (Fig. 35). Increasingly elaborate systems of pools, screens and nets were devised, with tame ducks to attract the wildfowl. Small dogs were trained to entice them to swim up the decoy pipes until they could be trapped. Such decoys became widespread along the Lancashire coast, in the Fens and the Somerset Levels and wherever suitable stretches of water could be adapted for the purpose. During the early eighteenth century Defoe commented on the decoys in Lincolnshire and along the Dorset coast, while manorial records frequently contain references to money spent on a decoy and the profits which arose from it.

The estate accounts of the Strangways family of Melbury (Dorset) provide evidence for their decoys at Abbotsbury (Dorset) and Compton Dundon (Somerset). In 1662 the steward spent £5 7s 0d at Abbotsbury on wages for the decoyman, food for his dogs, corn and hempseed for the decoy ducks and the occasional expense of employing men to break the ice on the decoy pool during the winter. Income from the decoy included 235 couple of ducks sold for £21 1s 11d, as well as 53 couple sent to Melbury for the family and an unspecified number presented as gifts to local gentlemen or to friends and relatives of the Strangways.

The Abbotsbury decoy continued to be profitable through the eighteenth and nineteenth centuries, and remains as a popular resort of wildfowl and a celebrated swannery. The remains of the decoy on the manor of Compton Dundon are clearly visible on aerial photographs, lying beside Decoy Farm. This decoy was constructed in 1695 at a cost of £139 9s 2½d, and contained five pipes or tunnels down which the wildfowl swam in their curiosity to observe the antics of the decoyman's well-trained dog. By the 1720s the decoy was making a regular annual profit of more than £35, and more than 2000 ducks were caught in it each year.

Many decoys were created throughout the Fens from the early seventeenth century. One of the most famous was Mucklemere in Wretham Park (Norfolk), which remained in use until the twentieth century. At Boarstall (Buckinghamshire) the eighteenth-century decoy is still in use; it now belongs to the National Trust, and the ducks captured in it are ringed and released in order to study their movements but it continues to be operated in the traditional manner, with tame ducks to encourage the wild ones to land and an artful dog to entice them into the pipes. Like deer parks, rabbit warrens, fishponds and dovecots, the decoys for wildfowl were essentially a manorial enterprise set up by landowners, and the survival of the relic features of so many former decoys is yet further evidence of the effect of estates upon the landscape.

## Formal gardens

As mentioned earlier, a remarkable account of the houses, parks, gardens and estates of the wealthy landowners of England at the

end of the seventeenth century is provided
by the accounts of her journeys made by the
intrepid and energetic traveller Celia
Fiennes during the years from 1685 to 1703.
As the well-connected member of a gentry
family she could gain access to many
establishments and as an inquisitive and
sharp-eyed visitor, could report on all
aspects of the estates and families she visited
in many parts of the country. From her
lively accounts of her travels the large
number of newly-built or recently enlarged
houses, with their carefully tended gardens
and parklands is very apparent, as is the
evidence for agricultural improvements,
forestry, industry and increasing trade. Her
narrative contains good descriptions of the
formal gardens which were so much in
fashion at the end of the century. At Oxford
in 1694 she visited New College and wrote
that

. . . the Garden was new makeing, there is a large
bason of water in the middle, there is little
walkes and mazes and round mounts for the
scholars to divert themselves in.

She also noted the gravel and grass walks,
and

a great mount in the middle of which is ascended
by degrees in a round of green paths deffended
by greens cutt low, and on the top is a summer
house, beyond these gardens is a bowling green,
and around it a close shady walke, walled
round . . .

At Oxford she was also impressed by the
Physic Garden where she thought 'the
variety of flowers and plants would have
entertained one a week'. When she visited
Warwick Castle in 1697 she noted the fine
formal gardens and the long avenues of
trees. She also encountered a problem to
which many visitors to castles and country
houses have fallen victim over the centuries,
and wrote that

at the entrance of the first Court the porter

diverts you with a history of Guy Earle of
Warwick . . .

At Burghley House in 1697 she observed
that 'it stands in a very fine parke which is
full of deer and fine rows of trees', and also
noted the gravel walks, grass squares with
statues, fountains, vineyard, warren and
groves with views over the whole parkland
'which makes its prospect very delightful'.
The fashion for formal gardens had clearly
spread to all parts of the country, but when
visiting Cornwall in 1698, Celia Fiennes was
less complimentary about the gardens she
saw. At Tregothnan, with its fine views
across Carrick Roads to Falmouth, the
Boscawen family had laid out a park with
long rows of trees in the approved manner
of the time, and a garden by the house in a
pattern of square beds, 'but the squares are
full of gooseberry and shrub-trees and looks
more like a kitchen garden'.

   In keeping with the ideas of her time, it
was artificially-contrived parkland and
gardens contrasting as much as possible
with the natural state which gained the
admiration of Celia Fiennes. At Ingestre
(Staffordshire) in 1698, for example, she was
greatly impressed by the long avenues of
Scots and Norway pine across the park, by
the well-trimmed yew trees, box hedges and
carefully barbered holly and laurel bushes,
by the flower garden divided into knots or
geometric patterns, and by the elegant
gravel walks, lodges and summer houses.[18]

   It was reaction against this excessive
formality which led Joseph Addison to
complain in *The Spectator* of 1712 that

British gardeners instead of humouring nature,
love to deviate from it as much as possible. Our
trees rise in cones, globes and pyramids. We see
the marks of the scissars upon every plant and
bush.

Views such as these were to lead to the
transformation of the estates of the gentry
during the next century.

# 5 The transformation of estate landscapes during the eighteenth century

During the eighteenth century the wealth and disposable income of aristocratic and gentry families increased enormously, and they could afford to indulge in grandiose schemes of garden design and landscaping on a scale hitherto undreamt of in England. They created the mansions, parks, gardens and carefully designed prospects which remain such a characteristic feature of so many English counties. Eighteenth-century agriculture in England became the most productive in the world, rents rose accordingly, and with additional income derived from military or naval service, political office, coal mines, rapidly increasing trade with all parts of the world, colonial plantations or investment in industry, the large landowners had wealth to lavish upon their estates and houses as never before. They also possessed the capital and technical knowledge to increase the productivity of their lands and some were a major force in promoting the agricultural advances of the century. By the end of the eighteenth century there were about 400 'great landlords' with a minimum annual income of £5000 and estates of at least 5000 acres. Many enjoyed considerably greater incomes, and owned very much larger acreages, making them by far the wealthiest group of men in the country.

There were also some 800 'greater gentry' possessing estates of from 3000 to 5000 acres, and below them a much larger group of some 4000 'lesser gentry' with smaller estates but still commanding incomes of from £1000 to £3000 a year. Together these estates occupied between a quarter and a third of all the cultivated land in England.[1]

The opulence and ostentation of life in the great houses contrasted starkly with the conditions of the poorly-paid and badly-housed labourers. Such inequality of wealth and living conditions was already great during the Middle Ages and increased during the sixteenth and seventeenth centuries, reaching its peak in the eighteenth century. In retrospect we can only marvel at the attitude of so many upright Christian gentlemen who were actively involved in local affairs, concerned about the fortunes of the country and apparently solicitous for the welfare of their tenants, and yet were complacent at the thought of spending many hundreds of pounds on a temple, grotto or sham medieval ruin to grace their grounds, and to have such structures built by labourers who were forced to support their families on wages which kept them barely above subsistence level.

## Avenues and plantations

Rising incomes coupled with the economic and political stability of the period meant that the eighteenth century saw the landed gentry at the height of their power and influence. Since their political and social status continued to be based on the ownership of land, on the prestige derived from an elegant country residence and on an ostentatious display of wealth and taste, landowners were willing to lavish ever-larger sums on the building and furnishings of their houses and on the gardens, parks and landscapes which surrounded them. For the first three decades of the eighteenth century the formal French or Dutch style of garden design, strongly influenced by the work at Versailles of Louis XIV's gardener, André le Nôtre (1613–1700), continued to hold sway, and numerous new English gardens were laid out in this fashion with geometrical parterres, terraces, walks, rectangular stretches of water or 'canals' and long straight avenues. These formal gardens required enormous labour in their maintenance; they demonstrated the contrast between the regulated paradise where Nature was tamed and the uncontrolled wilderness beyond the walls. The impact of the new parks and gardens upon the landscape, and especially of the long avenues of trees, was commented upon by observers and travellers such as Celia Fiennes and Daniel Defoe (mentioned above), and during the 1720s Defoe was greatly impressed by the change which was affecting the English countryside. 'The alteration is indeed wonderful throughout the whole kingdom', he wrote, and in Middlesex and Surrey he commented on the parks, 'the beauty and expense of which are only to be wondered at. . . . It is impossible to view these countries from any rising ground and not to be ravish'd with the delightful prospect'.[2]

By their nature gardens are one of the least permanent of art forms, and many of the formal gardens and planned landscapes of the early eighteenth century were swept away by the dramatic changes in fashion and taste which occurred later. We are therefore dependent on maps, prints and paintings for our knowledge of many of them. Particularly valuable are the engravings of

houses, parks and landscapes made by Leonard Knyff and John Kip, whose bird's-eye views of *c.*1700–1710, have already been noted as providing unique evidence of former garden layouts.

None the less, a few examples of this formal style do survive, notable among them Cirencester Park (Gloucestershire). During his very long life of 91 years, Allen, First Earl Bathurst (1684–1775) rebuilt his mansion at Cirencester and transformed the estate which consisted of 3000 exposed acres on the high Cotswolds into a wooded parkland, with carefully arranged plantations, crossed by a series of long rides or avenues, extending from the mansion at Cirencester to the extremity of the estate at Sapperton 8km (5 miles) away. In part his ideas may have derived from his friendship with the poet and gardener, Alexander Pope, who was an enthusiastic exponent of new ideas on landscaping and who had created at Twickenham a notable, small garden complete with grotto, shell temple, prospect mound and carefully arranged plantation of trees and shrubs.

Earl Bathurst's designs may have been partly fostered by his desire to rival the Duke of Beaufort's elaborate schemes at nearby Badminton, where the estate also spread over a large area of the Cotswolds and had been planted with vast numbers of trees creating long avenues stretching across the countryside and converging on a single point. Earl Bathurst added a focus to each vista he created by the clever use of classical temples, columns, sham castles and other romantic buildings and conceits. The main avenue of his park was focused on the fine tower of Cirencester church, just as the great avenue at Stowe (Buckinghamshire) led the eye to the steeple of Buckingham church 5km (3 miles) away. Another formal park landscape with a 5km (3 mile) long avenue was created at Wimpole (Cambridgeshire), and smaller examples of the elaborate formal style survive at Melbourne Hall

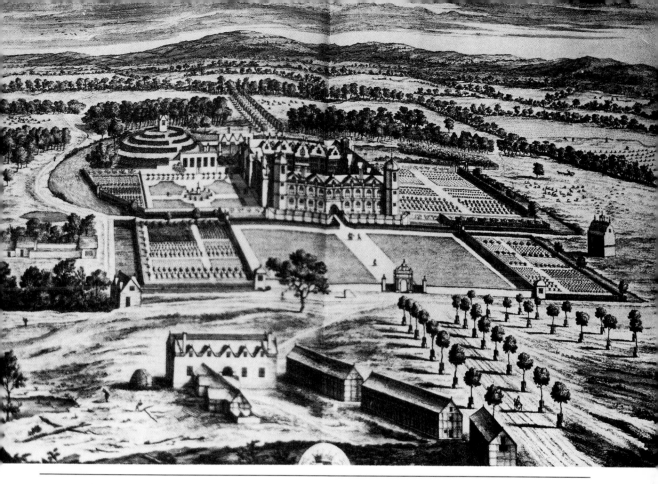

**36** *Dunham Massey (Cheshire). The mansion and formal garden with mount belonging to George Booth, Earl of Warrington. From Kip and Knyff,* Britannia Illustrata, *1709.*

(Derbyshire), Bramham Park (Yorkshire) created by Lord Bingley 1700–10, Dunham Massey (Cheshire) (Fig. 36) and St Paul's, Walden Bury (Hertfordshire) where the garden with its straight radiating walks, temples, pyramid and garden house remain although the house has been rebuilt. Melton Constable (Norfolk) had a 3km (2 mile) long avenue made up of four lines of trees, leading to a 'canal' or rectangular lake in front of it.

Ralph, first Duke of Montagu (1683–1709) had been Charles II's ambassador to France where he had visited the formal gardens and landscapes created for Louis XIV and had been especially impressed by the work of Le Nôtre at Versailles. Upon his return to England he employed a

Dutchman, Leonard van de Meulen, to remodel his estate at Boughton (Northamptonshire) and to create there a miniature Versailles, with formal parterres, terraces, fountains, rectangular stretches of water or 'canals', and elm avenues planted in straight lines across the surrounding countryside.

A partial but extremely interesting survival is the garden of the now-demolished mansion at Eastbury (Dorset) which was designed by Sir John Vanbrugh for George (Bubb) Doddington, the son of a Weymouth apothecary who inherited a vast fortune from an uncle and enjoyed a rapid rise to enormous wealth. The huge mansion was constructed between 1718 and 1738 and was said to have cost the sum of £140,000.

Soon after Bubb Doddington's death in 1762 much of the house was demolished. The gardens were laid out to the designs of Charles Bridgeman, the first of a new breed of professional garden designers, who was gardener to George I and who worked with Vanbrugh on the gardens and park layout at Castle Howard. The gardens at Eastbury were on a formal geometric plan, providing a view across the surrounding parkland, and used Bridgeman's favoured device of the 'ha-ha' or sunken fence to keep animals out and yet provide an unbroken prospect from the house to the plantations and a temple beyond. Included in the design were long beech and lime avenues, and two huge octagonal mounds or 'mounts', each 6m (20ft) high and 12m (40ft) across, which were topped by trees, while in the park beyond was a series of 14 smaller mounds, arranged in pairs, leading the eye across the landscape.

By the 1730s concepts of the ideal design were changing, and new ideas of naturalism, diversity, irregularity and surprises in the landscape were already being promoted. Young men with their education based almost entirely upon classical antiquity undertook the 'Grand Tour' through Europe and saw the paintings of artists such as Claude Lorrain, the brothers Nicolas and Gaspard Poussin, and Salvator Rosa. They returned to England ready to accept the new ideas being propounded by Joseph Addison in the *Spectator* and by Richard Steele in the *Guardian*, to abandon the formality of straight lines and narrow vistas, and to create the classical landscapes of the painters, complete with temples, monuments and ruins, on their own estates. As a result of this new enthusiasm for 'natural' scenery, the landscapes of estates all over the country were totally transformed as the old regularity was ruthlessly swept away, regardless of expense, and was replaced by a newly-created and extremely popular naturalism.[4]

## Professional landscapes

It is ironic that just as new mansions were being built and older houses transformed in the geometrical and symmetrical forms laid down by the Palladian style, vast labour and expense were also being devoted to creating surroundings which were totally informal, which shunned straight lines and where Gothic ruins, Chinese bridges and medieval grottoes jostled with Roman temples, classical sculptures, columns and obelisks. Examples of estates transformed in accordance with the new ideas included, on a large scale, those at Castle Howard, Blenheim, Chatsworth, Stowe, Petworth, Stourhead or Luton Hoo.

Work on more modest properties can also be seen, such as the poet William Shenstone's farm called the Leasowes near Halesowen (Worcestershire) or Philip Southcote's romantic *ferme ornée* at Woburn near Chertsey (Surrey), Lord Burlington's influential gardens at Chiswick House or Charles Hamilton's landscape at Pains Hill (Surrey) inspired by the paintings of Poussin. The new ideas, and the opportunities offered by the eagerness of landowners to execute them on their own estates, were seized upon by the three great landscape gardeners and designers of the century, William Kent (1685–1748), Lancelot 'Capability' Brown (1715–83) and Humphry Repton (1752–1818).

William Kent had been a painter and architect and had spent some years in Italy. His landscape designs were a reaction against the earlier fashion for formal gardens with elegant geometric shapes, neatly clipped box hedges and straight 'canals'. Kent introduced a much greater informality, using woodland, especially clumps of trees, as well as temples, obelisks and statues to break up a view or to create a pleasing vista. He made a conscious attempt to design landscapes like a painter and after the manner of Italian painting and theatre design; he popularized the classical idea of temples and columns, and introduced picturesque ruins and ornamental arches to improve the vista or to catch the eye. Much of his work was remodelled by later owners and landscape designers, and only the garden at Rousham (Oxfordshire), which he laid out for the owner General James Dormer from 1738, survives substantially as Kent planned it. Dormer was a friend of Pope and Swift, and was also a classical scholar and a collector of Italian bronzes. Kent remodelled the house and laid out the 10ha (25 acre) garden sloping down to the river Cherwell as a series of classical tableaux, each enclosed by carefully planted trees and complete with appropriate classical urns, statues, grottoes, temples and colonnades or with ruined Gothic chapel and ornamental arches, cascades and pools fed by winding streams.[5]

## 'Capability' Brown and Humphry Repton

The idea of informality as well as of total reconstruction of a landscape to achieve an ideal form was taken even further by Capability Brown who achieved enormous popularity and renown, and with amazing industry and dedication, worked for estate owners all over England, redesigning nearly 200 major parks and estates and changing the face of the countryside in many parts of England. Brown's work included the design of parks at Blenheim, Chatsworth, Luton Hoo, Petworth and Bowood. The characteristic features of his landscape designs included large, irregular stretches of ornamental water, clumps of trees, wide sweeps of lawn coming right up to the windows of the house and curving walks and driveways, all intended to enhance and emphasize the natural contours of the existing landscape.[6]

Humphry Repton drew up plans for more than 200 landscape gardens, in some places

altering or modifying the work of Brown or other earlier designers, reintroducing flower-beds, terraces and walks around the house and foreshadowing Victorian ideas with his conservatories, shrubberies and gravel paths (Figs 37–38). For the benefit of his clients, Repton incorporated his ideas and suggestions into beautifully-bound *Red Books* showing by the clever use of flaps and overlays how the existing scenery, gardens, parks or woodland could be improved (Fig. 38). His major commissions included Attingham (Shropshire), Ashridge (Hertfordshire), Cobham (Kent), Harewood (Yorkshire), Holkham (Norfolk), Longleat (Wiltshire) and Panshanger (Hertfordshire).

At the end of his career Repton summed up his views of the creation of ideal landscapes in his book *Fragments on the Theory and Practice of Landscape Gardening*, published in 1816. In it he criticized the early fashions represented by Capability Brown, 'I fully agree . . . in condemning that bald and insipid custom, introduced by Brown, of surrounding a house by a naked grass field'; and also disparaged the new craze for sham medieval style, 'we see buildings of every description, from the villa to the pigstye, with little pointed arches, or battlements, to look like Gothic; and a Gothic dairy is now become as common an appendage to a place, as were formerly the hermitage, the grotto, or the Chinese pavilion.'[7]

In spite of Repton's comments, however, Gothic continued throughout the nineteenth century to be regarded as the most appropriate style for estate cottages, farms, schools and almshouses, as well as for most churches. The work of the giants among landscape designers and improvers was supplemented by a host of others, amateur and professional, as the owners of estates from the greatest to the most modest sought to adopt the latest ideas. The cost and physical labour involved in many of the schemes, the reshaping of hills, the

**37**   *Beaudesert (Staffordshire), before improvement. From Humphry Repton* Fragment on the Theory and Practice of Landscape Gardening *1816*.

excavation of lakes and the planting of thousands of trees and the employment of whole armies of workmen, shows the great wealth of many landowners. It also illustrates the total confidence and assurance with which they were prepared to sweep away the elaborately laid out gardens, plantations, buildings and landscapes of their predecessors. Convinced of the superiority of their own taste, they used the landscape of their estates to create their own vision of an ideal countryside.

Capability Brown dammed rivers, created lakes, removed hillsides, planted huge numbers of trees and transformed the surroundings of many houses. At Blenheim he created the magnificent lake by damming the river Glyme and transformed the appearance of the 1012ha (2500 acre) park.[8] At Burghley from 1756 he totally altered the appearance of the grounds, destroying the formal garden by the house with its straight walks and clipped hedges, and laying down a large expanse of lawn which came right up to the walls of the house. The intended effect of making the house and parkland appear as a single entity was enhanced by sunken fences which kept the cattle out but did not interrupt the vista. The distant view was improved by clumps of trees and by a new lake of 13ha (32 acres) complete with an elegant stone bridge.[9]

No expense was spared and no trace of earlier fashion was allowed to survive as landowners rushed to outshine each other in their eagerness to adopt the latest ideas and create the new vision of an ideal countryside. At Longleat, Capability Brown entered into an agreement in 1757 to redesign the large formal gardens around the house with their elaborate parterres, terraces and clipped alleys. By 1759 the ground had been levelled, lawns laid down, a dam thrown across the nearby stream and a huge lake created. New roads were cut through the park and vast numbers of trees were planted, transforming both the landscape and the immediate surroundings of the house at the cost of some £6000.

The labour involved in such projects was great and the costs were high. Brown received £21,500 for his work on the park at Blenheim, £11,750 for his first contract at Petworth and £10,000 for landscaping at Luton Hoo. His work at Bowood (Wiltshire), including the creation of the lawns and great lake cost £4300. The laying out of the grounds and the construction of a lake at Clumber (Nottinghamshire) between 1774 and 1789 cost £6612; while at Doddington (Gloucestershire) the great fortune made by the Codrington family as sugar merchants and plantation owners enabled them to employ James Wyatt to build a new mansion and lay out the grounds in a lavish style, spending more

**38**  *Beaudesert: Repton's suggestions for improvement.*

than £4000 each year between 1797 and 1805.[10] The expense could sometimes be kept in check by using estate labour on the projects, but even so formidable amounts of money were often spent. At Corsham (Wiltshire) Brown's account for fees and services for the major work which he undertook on the grounds was as follows

To wit the making the great walks and sunke fence between the house and the Chippenham road.

The draining the ground between the sunk fence and the line of the garden.

To making the water in the parks, as also the levelling round it.

The levelling round the House, as also on front the New Building

The sunke fence on the front of the churchyard

All the planting included Mr Methuen to find trees and alterations which have been made in the Garden

The above articles comes to £1020 – 0 – 0.

Brown had already designed the picture gallery at Corsham Court to house Sir Paul Methuen's notable collection, and his landscape work had the effect of creating a pastoral view from the gallery windows in place of the previous stone walls and field system crossed by public footpaths and lanes. Later in the eighteenth century Humphry Repton also worked on the grounds at Corsham Court. He enlarged the park, altered the course of the turnpike road so that it was further from the house, broke up the surface of the old road and planted a screen of trees along it, and enlarged the lake. He also undertook an extensive programme of tree planting in the park. Accounts from local nurserymen between 1797 and 1799 detail the supply of:

   2700 oaks
1550 Spanish chestnuts
   600 English elms
1450 beeches
   100 sycamores

The cost of his work, not including the purchase of saplings, amounted to £2110.[11]

These huge costs for the major engineering and hydraulic feats involved in some landscape projects were, on many estates, dwarfed by the enormous expense of rebuilding, enlarging or totally altering the house together with its furnishing and decoration. Even the sums spent on park walls and garden buildings such as temples, grottoes, gazebos and summer houses were staggeringly large. The wall around the park and garden around Blenheim, more than 16km (10 miles) in length, cost some £1000 a mile during the early eighteenth century, and the Duke of Marlborough spent £200,000 on the grounds between 1760 and 1820.

Expensive mausoleums were also built for family burials on estates including Brocklesby (Lincolnshire), Bowood (Wiltshire), Wentworth Woodhouse (Yorkshire), West Wycombe (Buckinghamshire), Blickling (Norfolk) and Trentham Park (Staffordshire), culminating in the royal mausoleum of the 1860s in Windsor Park. Such elaborate burial chambers are another feature of the impact of gentry estates upon the landscape, enabling the estate owner to demonstrate his classical learning and rationalist theology and to dominate the surrounding countryside, even in death. The huge, impressive mausoleum at Castle Howard (Fig. 39), designed by Nicholas Hawksmoor, took many years to build and cost several thousand pounds.

Attingham Hall (Shropshire) provides another illustration of the lengths to which landscape designers and their wealthy patrons were prepared to go in order to

**39** *Castle Howard (Yorkshire). The magnificent mausoleum, designed by Nicholas Hawksmoor and built during the 1730s.*

**40** *Shobdon (Herefordshire). The Norman chancel arch and two finely-carved doorways from the twelfth-century church which was demolished by the Hon. Richard Bateman in c.1750 and replaced by a new Gothick church. The arches were re-erected as a romantic feature of the landscaped grounds of Shobdon Court.*

create their vision of the ideal surroundings to a house, artificially and expensively constructed yet apparently natural. The hall had been designed for the first Lord Berwick during the 1780s, and was the grandest house in Shropshire. It was situated beside the river Tern and close to the former site of a major ironworks and forge, which until 1757 had produced iron hoops, rods, nails and wire, as well as steel and brass. The extensive works by the river, together with the dwellings which had housed some 40 men and their families were demolished, and the site cleared, although some of the furnace pools were later used as part of the park landscape.

During the 1790s the second Lord Berwick, who was a connoisseur and collector of Italian paintings, employed Humphry Repton to model the landscape of his park according to the ideals of art. Repton's ideas for the park were set out in his *Red Book* of 1797, still kept at Attingham Park which now belongs to the National Trust. His suggestions, illustrated by views showing the effect his proposals would have, included plantations of trees against

**41** *Croome D'Abitot church (Worcestershire). Built on a new site in 1763 as a feature of the grounds of Croome Court by Lord Coventry. The interior of the church is filled with the large monuments of the Coventry family, many removed from the demolished medieval parish church.*

which the house might be viewed to best
advantage, the removal of barns and
outbuildings, the diversion of the river and
the creation of a dam, cascade and elegant
bridges, the diversion of the nearby road and
the building of lodges to give distinction to
the park entrance, and the careful siting of
trees so as to create panoramic views from
the house to the Wrekin and the distant
Welsh mountains. Many of these
suggestions were carried out, creating one of
the finest of English parks, although even
Lord Berwick did not adopt Repton's idea of
adding a spire to the tower of Wroxeter
church to form the focus for one of the
views from the house.[12]

Fortunately, in their desire to realize their
vision of an ideal landscape few landowners
were prepared to go as far as Richard
Bateman of Shobdon (Herefordshire) (Fig.
40) who in 1752–6 rebuilt a notable Norman
church in the 'correct' Gothic style, and used
the magnificently carved Romanesque
arches to provide a hilltop viewpoint at the
end of the avenue leading from his mansion.

At Croome D'Abitot (Worcestershire),
where Lord Coventry built a mansion
during the 1750s, the landscaping by
Capability Brown involved the demolition
of the parish church, which was rebuilt on
the hillside above the house, providing an
attractive feature of the park (Fig. 41). Like
so many other 'estate' churches, the interior
of Croome D'Abitot is overwhelmed by the
large monuments of the Coventry family;
but in the churchyard are the headstones
erected by the family to various servants
including a valet, a gamekeeper and
a steward. The churchyards at
Belton (Lincolnshire), Sherborne
(Gloucestershire), Crowcombe (Somerset)
and many others are notable for the number
of memorials to family servants, many
recording very long years of devoted service
and indicating the high esteem in which such
servants were held. At Bulmer on the Castle
Howard estate, a monument to Christopher

Thomas 1748, records that he 'wrought in
brass and iron for forty-five years for the
third and fourth Earls of Carlisle'.

## Stourhead, Fonthill and Stowe

Two spectacular examples of the way in
which, given sufficient wealth, the whole
landscape could be altered and moulded to
suit the taste of the owners survive in south-
west Wiltshire. One is at Stourhead, where
the wealthy banker, Henry Hoare, began to
lay out the grounds and adapt the landscape
in the valley below his house in about 1741.
During the following 30 years, landscaping,
the creation of a lake, the planting of
innumerable trees and shrubs, and the
erection of bridges, temples, grottoes, a
boat-house, obelisk, ruined 'convent' and
other buildings and garden features of all
sorts continued. The result is one of the
most beautiful pieces of artificial countryside
ever created, contrived so skilfully that it
appears completely natural.

The other example is William Beckford's
extravaganza at Fonthill. Here, at the end of
the eighteenth century, the inordinately
wealthy eccentric and connoisseur, William
Beckford, demolished the great Palladian
mansion, Fonthill Splendens, which had
been built by his father in c. 1760, and
employed James Wyatt to create a fantastic
Gothic folly, a huge cruciform building
107m (350ft) by 88m (290ft) with an
octagonal tower, 68m (225ft) high, at the
crossing. This was the so-called Fonthill
Abbey (Fig. 43). The great tower collapsed
in 1825 and most of the rest of the building
has been demolished, but the extravagant
landscaping remains, the vast woodlands
planted by Beckford, with lakes, temples,
grottoes, boat-houses, an ice-house,
elaborate gateways and a great wall of cut
stone several miles long enclosing the whole
inner estate. Both Stourhead and Fonthill
show the dramatic effect which enormous

**42** *Warkworth Castle (Northumberland). Hermitage complete with eighteenth-century hermit addressing visitors in the grounds of the castle. The late-medieval hermitage contained spacious accommodation and a chapel. From Thomas Hearne,* Antiquities of Great Britain, *1776.*

wealth coupled with dedication could have upon the landscape.[13]

An even more remarkable example is Stowe (Buckinghamshire) where Sir Richard Temple, later Viscount Cobham, began to lay out the grounds around his mansion in 1713. Thereafter Bridgeman and Kent were both employed on the work, Capability Brown served there as under-gardener, and alterations continued to be made to the grounds throughout the rest of the century. The first formal layout was later abandoned and replaced with the more popular naturalistic style during the 1730s, and the area of the garden grew even larger,

eventually covering 162ha (400 acres), until it became what has been described as the largest work of art in the country. The feature which above all distinguishes Stowe is the number of surviving garden buildings, temples, monuments, bridges, gateways and other structures, nearly 40 in all; others which once existed have been demolished or have disappeared. The leading architects of the day were employed in their design, including Vanbrugh, Kent, Gibbs, Adam and the amateur architect and relative of the Temple-Grenville family, Thomas Pitt, First Lord Camelford; likewise, leading sculptors such as Nost, Scheemakers and

**43**  *Fonthill Splendens (Wiltshire). The mansion was built and the grounds landscaped by Alderman William Beckford c.1760. In 1807 the mansion was demolished by his son, also William, who was building the fantastic Gothick folly, Fonthill Abbey, on a hilltop overlooking the surrounding countryside.*

Rysbrack were commissioned to supply statues and monuments for the garden, regardless of expense.[14]

## Ornamental buildings

Few landowners wished or could afford to emulate the scale of this extravagance, or could afford to overload their grounds with ornamental buildings as at Stowe, but many followed the prevailing fashion for temples, sham ruins, towers, monuments and grottoes. One of the finest of all grottoes is at Goldney House (Bristol) and was built by Thomas Goldney, a Quaker merchant, in 1739 (Fig. 44). The ground was excavated to

create a large underground chamber, into which a stream was made to run, and the walls and roof were lined with shells, coral and sparkling stones, and niches held statues of lions and the god Neptune.

Here the owner and his friends might enjoy romantic thoughts or sombre reflections, or might congratulate themselves on the classical learning which

**44**  *Goldney House, Clifton, Bristol. Interior of the shell-lined grotto of c.1739. Built by the Quaker merchant, Thomas Goldney, as one of the features of his notable garden. (G. Kelsey.)*

45 *Rievaulx (Yorkshire). Doric temple, part of the landscape features built on Rievaulx terraces above the abbey ruins by Thomas Duncombe of Duncombe Park c.1758.*

enabled them to appreciate the allusions and concepts which grottoes, like sham castles, spurious medieval ruins or other similar follies represented. The Goldney grotto, together with the elegant formal garden in which it is situated, is a fine example of the thought, care and wealth which was devoted to such ends and of the total control which wealthy landowners could exercise over their property.[15]

Copies of Greek (Figs 45 and 46) and Roman temples, Gothic ruins, grottoes, arbours, triumphal arches and the like demonstrated the owner's culture, taste, classical education, literary knowledge or romantic sensibility, but were not really practical for the English climate. Horace Walpole described an evening entertainment arranged before the grotto in the grounds of Stowe during the summer of 1770. The romance of the evening was spoilt by the fact that 'The evening was more than cool, and the destined spot anything but dry'. The elegant party, which included Princess Amelia, sister of George III, was 'wrapped up in cloaks and great coats for fear of catching cold', and a fellow-guest recalled that Walpole had called out for cherry brandy on returning to the house in order to ward off the cold. But all over the country estate owners were not deflected from their romantic dreams or deterred by practical realities from continuing to erect buildings suitable only for a Mediterranean climate.[16]

## Tree-planting

The landscape alterations of the eighteenth and early nineteenth centuries included the planting of great numbers of trees and shrubs, transforming the appearance of much of the English countryside, and giving the landscape a new character which has survived into the late twentieth century. For landowners the planting of trees on their estates had three advantages. It would in time produce profitable timber for sale and for use on the estate, it was an essential component of the idealized landscape which was so much desired, and the woodland provided shelter for the foxes and game whose pursuit became such an addiction among country gentlemen.

Estate records of the later eighteenth century provide abundant evidence of the huge number of trees planted. For the

46 *Rievaulx (Yorkshire). Ionic temple.*

woodland around his new mansion at Castle Howard the Earl of Carlisle had large saplings sent by ship and barge from London via Scarborough or Bridlington, and in 1704, for example, he ordered '600 limes, 300 chestnuts and 60 English Elms, they must be about eight foot high, good fresh trees'. At Holkham during the last twenty years of the eighteenth century no fewer than 2,123,090 saplings were planted on some 291ha (720 acres) of the estate, of 49 different varieties.[17] At Bowood during the mid-eighteenth century the Earl of Shelburne regularly planted 150,000 saplings each year, mostly of oak. On the Welbeck estate (Nottinghamshire) of the Duke of Portland, 24–32ha (60–80 acres) and sometimes 40ha (100 acres) of woodland were newly planted each year, using oak, beech, larch, Spanish chestnut, Weymouth pine and other conifers. Sales of timber and coppice wood accounted for some 10 per cent of the income of the Longleat estate in Wiltshire during the late eighteenth century and the woodlands were carefully managed. Many thousands of saplings were planted each year, and the income from timber sales rose from £1652 in 1779 to £4878 in 1807. On their estate at Brocklesby (Lincolnshire) between 1787 and 1889 six generations of the Yarborough family planted over 17 million trees, transforming the character of the whole landscape. In 1849 the landmark and memorial known as Pelham's Pillar, a square tower 39m (128ft) high, was built near Caistor on the highest point of the estate to commemorate the achievement of Charles Anderson Pelham, First Baron Yarborough (1748–1823) in planting over 12 million trees on his lands.[18]

It was not only very wealthy landowners who were interested in tree-planting. On a more modest scale James Frampton of Moreton (Dorset) and his son, also James, were greatly concerned with their woodlands, both as a commercial undertaking and as an adornment to their estate. They planted thousands of saplings and totally changed the previously bleak appearance of that part of Dorset, keeping a careful record of all the trees they planted. They planted fir, larch, birch, chestnut, oak, ash, maple, beech and other species, and James the Younger, wrote a long doggerel-verse poem giving detailed instruction on the art of tree-planting. The number of saplings planted each year was impressive, as the following figures from their notebooks show:

| *Saplings planted* | |
|---|---|
| 1781 | 130,800 |
| 1783 | 222,205 |
| 1791 | 27,120 |
| 1792 | 25,000 |
| 1793 | 46,560 |
| 1794 | 68,655 |
| 1795 | 139,059 |
| 1796 | 88,464 |
| 1797 | 45,166 |
| 1798 | 63,373 |
| 1799 | 52,313 |
| 1800 | 70,472 |

It is to landowners like the Framptons and the many other similarly-minded country gentlemen that the present woodland cover of so much of the English countryside is due.[19]

To cater for the rapidly-growing demand for saplings as well as for shrubs, garden plants, flowers and seeds, a new profession of nurseryman and seedsman developed, and the desire for new species encouraged enterprising plant collectors to scour the world for new and exotic varieties. Among the introductions which had a great effect upon the parks and gardens of English estates was the Cedar of Lebanon which was introduced from Asia Minor during the later seventeenth century and gained popularity as a specimen tree. The horse chestnut and larch were also introduced about this time. During the eighteenth century introductions included the Lombardy poplar and the

Canada poplar, the Weymouth pine, the Acacia and the Virginia dogwood. From the early nineteenth century the choice of trees and shrubs grew rapidly, with the Douglas fir (1827), the Sitka spruce (1831), the Monterey cypress (1838), the Monkey Puzzle, which although introduced earlier only became widely available from *c.*1843, the Western Hemlock (1851) and Lawson's cypress (1854). A shrub which had a tremendous effect on parks and woodland was the rhododendron which was first imported from North America in 1809.[20]

## Fox-hunting

Another powerful influence in changing the appearance of the landscape during the eighteenth century was the obsession which many gentlemen developed for hunting and shooting. From the mid-eighteenth century fox-hunting became increasingly fashionable, especially in the Midland counties where Hugo Meynell during his long mastership of the Quorn from 1753 to 1800, created a pack of specially bred hounds which became famous for their speed and hunting ability. The Quorn was rapidly emulated by other Midland packs such as the Belvoir, Cottesmore, Pytchley, Grafton, Fitzwilliam and Lord Yarborough's famous pack at Brocklesby (Lincolnshire), while in the south-west packs such as the Duke of Beaufort's, the Berkeley, the Heythrop and Cotswold were developed, and by the end of the eighteenth century few parts of the country were not regularly hunted. The social effects of this phenomenal growth of interest in hunting, which throughout each winter absorbed much of the time of many of the leading county gentry, are outside the scope of this study, but the impact upon the landscape was remarkable.

Coverts or areas of gorse were deliberately planted where foxes could be encouraged to live and breed, and where they could readily be found by the hounds. Many of these coverts survive, often no more than a few acres in extent and commonly including undergrowth of laurel to provide shelter and seclusion. They can often be recognized in the landscape from their small size, irregular shape and position in odd corners or on land that defied cultivation; they also bear names such as Gorse, Spinney, Fox Covert, Fox Warren, Copse or Bushes, while the names of others reflect the date at which they were created, such as Trafalgar, Waterloo, Wellington, Canada, Bunkers Hill or Botany Bay. Notable examples in the Quorn country include Willoughby Gorse, north of Melton Mowbray, Walton Thorns, Hose Thorns and Clowson Thorns in Leicestershire. A few hunts even went to the trouble of creating artificial earths where foxes could breed.

The passion for hounds and horses led to the creation of elaborate kennels and stables adjacent to many country houses. One of the best examples is at Badminton (Gloucestershire) where the splendidly-appointed stables are built around all four sides of a large square courtyard, while beyond are the kennels for the foxhounds.

Daniel Defoe described the stables at Petworth (Sussex) as 'equal to some noblemen's whole houses'. Among many other notable stable buildings erected during the eighteenth century is the vast complex, including a riding school or covered exercise yard for horses, built for Lord Rockingham at Wentworth Woodhouse (Yorkshire) in 1768, or the stables arranged around a large quadrangle at Calke Abbey (Derbyshire). At Calke Abbey, as at many other mansions, the stable block of 1712 forms part of a collection of ancillary buildings and facilities including a carriage house, estate smithy, carpenters' shop, fire-engine house and estate yard, while beyond is the home farm and 3ha (7 acres) of walled kitchen garden.

Even among enthusiastic fox-hunters, not

all wanted their hounds kept so close to the house, and at Belvoir Castle (Leicestershire), for example, the stables adjoin the house, while the celebrated pack of hounds was housed nearly two miles away in kennels designed by James Wyatt. Likewise, at Shugborough the impressive stables are beside the house, but the kennels are in deep woodland a mile away. At Milton (Northamptonshire) the well-bred hounds of the Fitzwilliam hunt were housed in kennels built to resemble a medieval ruin and to form a feature of the park, and the hounds of the Berkeley hunt are kept in castellated kennels in the grounds of Berkeley Castle (Gloucestershire). At Iwerne Steepleton (Dorset) the kennels built *c.*1770 for Peter Beckford, the author of the popular *Thoughts upon Hare and Fox Hunting* (1781), have been turned into a row of cottages.[21]

From the later eighteenth century shooting also increased in popularity with the introduction of the breech-loading shot-gun with which game could be shot in flight. The demand for ever larger 'bags' of game meant that more and more pheasants were bred, and the specialist occupation of gamekeeper became increasingly important. At the same time the game was protected from the lower orders by ever more ferocious game laws, creating a widening gap between the gentry and the tenants and labourers on their estates and souring social relationships. Game preservation had an effect on the landscape similar to fox-hunting, in creating artificially planted coverts and shelters for the pheasants. The growth of interest and of expenditure upon game preservation and shooting can be seen from the following figures, relating to the Longleat estate: in 1790 expenditure on pheasant rearing was £264. By 1810 this figure had risen to £400. In 1856 it had reached a staggering £2555.[22]

## Agricultural improvements

As well as changing many parts of the countryside with their parks and gardens, major landowners did much to transform the landscape during the eighteenth century by their encouragement of agricultural improvements and commercial developments. It was clearly in the best interests of landowners to encourage their tenants to adopt the newest techniques and increase the productivity of their lands so that they could afford to pay higher rents. As in the previous century, therefore, many landowners took a leading role in enclosures, drainage, reclamation of marshland and heath, the extension of cultivation and in the introduction of new crops, livestock breeds and improved farming methods on their estates.

In particular, it was the major landowners who possessed the incentive as well as the drive and influence, to obtain Acts of Parliament for the enclosure of open fields and commons throughout the country during the eighteenth century. Landowners such as Jethro Tull experimented with seed drills, new ploughs, harrows, artificial fertilizers and methods of cultivation, while Robert Bakewell of Dishley (Leicestershire) and Thomas Coke of Holkham (Norfolk) carried out ambitious programmes of livestock improvement by selective breeding. It was landowners who took the lead in the establishment of the influential agricultural societies such as the Royal Society of Arts, 1758, the Bath and West of England Society, 1777, the Smithfield Club, 1798, the Board of Agriculture, 1793 and eventually the Royal Agricultural Society of England in 1838. All of these, and many smaller clubs and societies, helped to popularize and spread new ideas and improved practices.

Estate owners and their stewards were enthusiasts for the new agriculture, and without the encouragement and pressure which they provided the complex business of obtaining Enclosure Acts from Parliament and the heavy expense involved in surveying, allotting and fencing the lands would not have been carried through. It was also in the interests of landowners to have a smaller number of large leasehold farms and substantial farmers on their estates rather than deal with numerous smallholders, often with complex life tenures, low rents and ancient privileges. Many were scathing in their condemnation of cottagers who depended on common grazing land for their livelihood, especially during the Napoleonic War, when inflated corn prices meant that the land could be used much more profitably. William Mavor, a leading Berkshire farmer, wrote in 1813 that 'wherever there are large wastes and particularly near forests the lazy industry and beggarly independence of the lower orders of people who enjoy commons is a source of misery to themselves and of loss to the community'. Likewise, John Billingsley, a progressive Somerset farmer, expressed the same feelings in 1797:

moral effects of an injurious tendency accrue to the cottager, from a reliance on the imaginary benefits of stocking a common . . . In sauntering after his cattle he acquires a habit of indolence. . . . Day labour becomes disgusting; the aversion increases by indulgence and, at length, the sale of a half-fed calf or hog furnishes the means of adding intemperance to idleness.[23]

Over much of England, and especially in those areas where great estates predominated, such commons, common fields and common rights were swept away by enclosures, together with the irregular fields, dispersed holdings, winding trackways and ancient tenures. The effect upon the landscape was certainly dramatic. In much of the Midlands enclosures brought new permanent hedges and fences, replacing the bleak open fields and unobstructed views by a regular pattern of planned fields and roads with hedgerow trees giving a wooded appearance. In south-west England observers commented upon the extension of cultivated land, for example Defoe in 1724 wrote of the great areas of newly cultivated land on Salisbury Plain

But 'tis more remarkable still; how a great part of these downs comes by a new method of husbandry, to be not only made arable, which they never were in former days, but to bear excellent wheat, and great crops too . . .[24]

In the same way the agricultural writer, Arthur Young, described the changes which had been brought about in Norfolk, particularly by Thomas Coke of Holkham and Sir Robert Walpole of Houghton. Writing in 1768, Young commented that

All the country from Holkham to Houghton was a wild sheep-walk before the spirit of improvement seized the inhabitants; and this glorious spirit has wrought amazing effects; for instead of boundless wilds and uncultivated wastes, inhabited by scarce anything but sheep, the county is all cut up into inclosures, cultivated in a most husband-like manner.[25]

In the East Riding of Yorkshire during the late eighteenth century the largest landowner, Sir Christopher Sykes of Sledmere, brought about a similar transformation of the landscape. A contemporary observer commented that Sykes

By assidulty and perseverance in building and planting and enclosing the Yorkshire wolds in the short space of 30 years set such an example to other owners of land, as has caused what was once a bleak and barren tract of country to become now one of the most productive and best cultivated districts in the county of York.

In Staffordshire the Leveson-Gower family, later Dukes of Sutherland, had made a vast fortune from Wolverhampton industries and Staffordshire coal mines, and owned a large estate at Trentham, as well as vast properties in Scotland. The first Duke (1758–1833) ruthlessly evicted his Scottish tenants and cleared the land for sheep farming, while on his English estates he employed a Scottish land-agent, James Loch, to compel his Staffordshire tenants to adopt new methods and new tenures. He was responsible for constructing farmsteads and many miles of new access roads and underground drains, making new enclosures with quickset hedges, introducing new livestock breeds, new arable crops and vastly improving the productivity of the land. The huge monument to the first Duke set on a giant column erected in 1836, still dominates the park at Trentham and the surrounding landscape.

A notable example from the south-west of a family whose interest in agricultural improvement totally transformed their large estate is the Aclands of Killerton (Devon) and Selworthy (Somerset). During the late eighteenth century Sir Thomas Acland was in the forefront of the movement to introduce new trees and shrubs into England. He employed the young Scotsman, John Veitch, to landscape his park and encouraged Veitch to set up as a nurseryman and to employ William and Thomas Lobb and numerous others to scour the world for new plants. Throughout the nineteenth century the Aclands continued this tradition of concern for their park and gardens and enthusiasm for agricultural innovation. The eleventh baronet, Sir Thomas Dyke Acland, was a leading member of the Bath and West of England Agricultural Society and editor of its influential *Journal*. He also wrote an important essay 'On the Farming of Somersetshire' which was published in the *Journal* in 1850, and was active in rebuilding farmsteads, carrying out enclosures and encouraging improved methods on the farms throughout the estate.

In the royal forest of Exmoor, the wealthy Worcestershire ironmaster, John Knight, bought some 10,000 acres of the most remote and desolate part of the moorland from the Crown in 1818 for the enormous sum of £50,000. The area was a desert, devoid of roads, hedges, trees or farms, but John Knight and his son, Frederic Winn Knight, reclaimed much of this unpromising land for agriculture, pouring in vast sums of money for drainage, sub-soiling, road-building, the application of lime and fertilizers, and the building of farms, converting all but the most inaccessible hilly or waterlogged areas into productive land and creating the present landscape of Exmoor.[26]

Throughout the whole of England there was a rapid and total transformation of the landscape. Straight new roads, often 12m (40ft) wide, and regular new fields were laid out by the enclosure commissioners, and on many estates the opportunity was taken to build isolated farmsteads in the midst of the fields. These new farms often provide clear evidence of estate ownership. Most were built during the early nineteenth-century period of agricultural prosperity, with solid well-planned buildings replacing the haphazard arrangement of earlier farmsteads. Many include large barns (Fig. 47), good cattle housing and stables, and incorporate a circular shed to accommodate a horse-wheel which was used to provide power for threshing machines, turnip and straw cutting or for mixing food for cattle and pigs. Individual estates commonly had their own easily recognisable styles of architecture, while others have coats of arms, date stones or the initials of the estate-owner prominently displayed. The date at which such farms were founded is often evident from their names which reflect the events or battles of the Napoleonic War, such as Trafalgar, Quatre Bras, Hougemont, Normandy, Wellington and Waterloo.

On estates throughout the country examples of these early nineteenth-century

**47** *Castle Barn, Great Badminton (Gloucestershire). One of a group of three farmsteads designed by Thomas Wright for the fourth Duke of Beaufort. (Colin Miller.)*

farms may be seen. At Alnwick most of the Duke of Northumberland's farms were rebuilt during this period; at Badminton, somewhat earlier, the Duke of Beaufort employed the architect and landscape designer Thomas Wright to design several farms including some disguised as castles or Gothic ruins with battlements, towers, pointed arches, and other mock-medieval features. Other landowners, carried along by the optimism of high corn prices during the Napoleonic War, were not slow to follow these examples. One of the best-documented estates where the rebuilding process can be studied in detail is Holkham (Norfolk) which was inherited by Thomas Coke, later first Earl of Leicester, in 1776, and managed by him until his death in 1842. Using Samuel Wyatt as his architect, Coke systematically rebuilt all the farms on the estate, including the Home Farm with its great barn which was used for his famous

'Sheep Shearings'. Shortly before his death he claimed, perhaps with some exaggeration, that he had spent half a million pounds on farm buildings; certainly he had spent enormous sums, using bricks from his own yard and building on a solid and totally self-confident scale.[27]

Enclosures, land drainage and improved farm buildings were greatly to the advantage of landlords, since rents could be substantially increased. Following enclosures rents were commonly doubled or trebled, but the new large farms which were created, often several hundred acres in extent, and the fine new farmhouses and buildings, required a new sort of tenant, reliable, efficient and with sufficient capital to stock and work the enlarged farm. Improvements, therefore, contributed to the further polarization of rural society, widening the gulf between the landlords and their substantial tenants on the one hand and the mass of poorly-paid labourers along with their families on the other.

## Roads and canals

Landowners took a major part in improvements in communications during the eighteenth century, securing Acts of Parliament for the creation of turnpike roads, and encouraging improvements in navigation and the creation of canals. For example, it was a group of landowners led by Ralph Allen of Prior Park (Bath) who carried forward the improvement of the river Avon in 1727, making it possible for barges to ply between Bristol and Bath and stimulating the trade in coal and building stone. In 1761 the Duke of Bridgewater's canal was opened connecting his coal mines at Worsley with the rapidly-expanding industries of Manchester. In 1779–80 the Marquess of Rockingham employed William Jessop to make the Greaseborough Cut to the river Don so that coal could be transported from his estate at Wentworth Woodhouse (Yorkshire). It was landowners as well as industrialists who provided the finance for the Grand Trunk Canal (1776–77) between the Mersey and the Trent, and the Thames and Severn Canal with its remarkable Sapperton tunnel (1789), more than 3km (2 miles) long through the Cotswolds.

Later and even more dramatic canal schemes, as well as port improvements, depended heavily on the financial backing of local landowners, especially those who sought to exploit the mineral resources of their estates. The Willoughbys of Nottingham made their fortune from coal mining, the Fullers of Heathfield (Sussex) took a leading part in the iron-founding and cannon-making industry of the Weald, the Lowthers exploited their coal mines in Cumberland, the Leveson-Gower family of Trentham (Staffordshire) owed their fortune

to coal and iron-working industries in the Black Country, while the exploitation of tin and copper in Cornwall, lead in the Pennines and Derbyshire, coal in South Wales and Yorkshire, all depended upon the support of the gentry families who owned the mineral rights.[28] The Duke of Northumberland's income from his collieries rose from £2255 in 1790 to £13,215 by 1813 and reached £23,400 in 1831; while a major part of the large revenues of the Bishop of Durham and of the Dean and Chapter of Durham cathedral which derived from their vast landed estates came from the leases granted to coal miners.

Landowners greatly influenced the routes taken by the canals and the style of canal architecture. In Hertfordshire the building of the Grand Junction Canal, making a direct waterway connection between London and Birmingham, was authorized by Act of Parliament in 1793. Where the canal passes through Cassiobury Park the towpath was made to cross from the west to the east bank because the Earl of Essex feared that poachers might otherwise gain easy access to his game preserves. An elegant bridge was also built with fine stonework and balustrades to carry his driveway over the canal. Where the Trent and Mersey canal passed through the estate of the wealthy pottery-owner Josiah Wedgwood at Etruria (Staffordshire), the waterway was widened to form an ornamental feature for the mansion, and at Tixall (Staffordshire) the canal was formed into a lake from which a lawn sloped up to the now-demolished Tixall Hall.

On the Kennet and Avon Canal, which opened in 1810 enabling barges to carry goods and passengers between Bath and London, several fine bridges were constructed where the waterway passed through gentry estates. At Wilcot near Pewsey (Wiltshire) the landowner, Lady Wroughton, only agreed to the construction of the canal through her land when the canal company undertook to widen the cutting to form an ornamental lake and to build a highly-decorated bridge specially designed by their engineer and architect, John Rennie, and which is now known as 'Ladies Bridge'. At its highest point the Kennet and Avon Canal passes through the Bruce Tunnel beneath Savernake Forest, the estate of the Brudenell-Bruce family, Earls of Ailesbury, and the tunnel entrances are suitably ornate and carry memorial plaques to members of the family. Likewise, the Sapperton tunnel, which took the Thames and Severn Canal under the highest point of the Cotswolds and beneath part of the Bathurst estate, was provided with appropriately impressive portals at each end.[29]

## The office of steward

In the running of their estates, relationships with tenants, collection of rents and a host of other business, ranging from the organization of charities to the securing of votes at parliamentary elections, landowners relied heavily on the services of their stewards or agents. The office developed from the bailiffs, surveyors and stewards who had served the great medieval households, and by the eighteenth century the estate agent or steward was an indispensible feature of most large estates. Daniel Eaton, who was land steward to the third Earl of Cardigan at Deene (Northamptonshire) between 1725 and 1732, was invaluable in running this large landed estate, especially since Lord Cardigan was frequently absent, and Eaton's letters to his master give a vivid account of the administration of the Earl's widespread lands in Northamptonshire and Leicestershire, as well as of all aspects of life on the estate.[30]

Likewise, on the Longleat estate of the Marquess of Bath centred on Wiltshire but comprising more than 50,000 acres and extending to Somerset, Gloucestershire, Herefordshire and Shropshire, almost all aspects of estate management were left to the stewards Thomas Davies (steward 1779–1807) and his son, also Thomas, (steward 1807–39).[31] A few stewards became notable innovators themselves. John Ellman (1753–1832) of Glynde (Sussex) was a tenant farmer and also steward to the Trevor family of Lewes. He was a leading breeder of Southdown sheep, a regular contributor to agricultural journals, active in drainage and enclosure schemes and a founder-member of the Smithfield Society and the Sussex Agricultural Society. He served as Deputy-Lieutenant of Sussex during the years of agricultural depression and distress following the Napoleonic War.[32]

Some indication of the importance of these agents and of the respect in which they were held by the landowners can be seen in the monuments to them in parish churches. An example from the seventeenth century survives in the church at Tormarton (Gloucestershire) and illustrates the diligent services of a bailiff, his care for the efficient administration of the estate, concern for his master's interests and pride in the crucial part he played in a great enterprise. When Gabriel Russell died in 1663 his family had administered the Marquess of Newcastle's estates in Gloucestershire for nearly a century.

> Here Gabriel Russell lies
> Whose watchful eyes
> Were William, Marquess of Newcastle's spies.
> Over three parishes his onlie hands
> Were here entrusted with his lordship's lands,
> Full ninty yeares my Father and I
> Were sarvants to that nobillyty.
> But all that knew them did them witness bare
> Of their just dealing loyalty and care
> And for their comfort here below
> One and twenty children could they show
>
> Who deceased the 27 day of December 1663
> His age was 88 yeares.

A final example from the eighteenth century of the effect which a landowner could have upon his estate and the total assurance with which he could impose a radical change upon it comes from the parishes of Halstock and Corscombe (Dorset). During the later eighteenth century most of the lands in these parishes were owned by Thomas Brand Hollis. He was inspired by the ideas of Greek and Roman philosophy, by English reformers and advocates of political and religious freedom and by the writings of contemporaries such as Rousseau to change the names of the farms and fields on his estate.

Although this did not affect the landscape of the district, it has left an abiding memorial to the landowner. His new farm names include Liberty, Milton, Harrington, Marvell, Ludlow and Sydney while with total disregard for the broad vowels of his Dorset tenants Hollis renamed all the fields after his heroes such as Socrates, Solon, Aristotle, Cicero, Plutarch, Pythagoras, Knox, Cromwell, Lilburn, Bastwick and Pym.[33]

# 6 Paternalism and despotism: estate villages, farms and cottages

The attitude displayed by landowners to the tenants and servants living on their estates during the eighteenth and nineteenth centuries ranged from benevolence and genuine concern for the plight of the needy and unfortunate to harsh indifference and demand for total subordination. As was shown in Chapter 5, the desire for privacy, seclusion and a spreading parkland appropriate to their rank and station led many gentry families to surround their houses with idealized landscapes, apparently natural but contrived at great expense. This in turn led to the re-routing of roads and paths, the demolition of cottages or farms, the re-siting of churches, and in some cases even the total removal of villages.

## The diversion of roads

The closure of roads which had formerly passed undesirably close to mansions was very common during the eighteenth

**48** *Castle Howard (Yorkshire). The Pyramid Gate designed by Sir John Vanbrugh and erected in 1719 to provide an appropriately imposing entrance to the estate.*

century, and examples may be seen in all parts of the country where, heedless of the inconvenience caused to travellers, roads have been obliged to follow new routes around park walls in order to provide peace and solitude for the inhabitants of the mansion within. For instance at Apethorpe (Northamptonshire) the main road to Peterborough, which had formerly run right past the house, was diverted several miles around the park by the Earl of Westmorland during the 1740s. At Panshanger (Hertfordshire) some 10km (6 miles) of new road were constructed around the estate of Earl Cowper to replace those which had been closed in 1801 to provide seclusion for the house.[1]

When Capability Brown redesigned the grounds of Harewood House (Yorkshire), the turnpike road from York to Skipton was diverted to a new route around the park; while in Staffordshire the Stafford to Lichfield road was diverted away from the newly enlarged mansion and park at Shugborough by Thomas Anson, who owned the estate from 1720 to 1773.[2]

At Corsham Court (Wiltshire) Humphry Repton, as part of his work to remodel the park, extended the northern boundary by 45ha (110 acres), diverting the London to Bath turnpike road beyond the new enclosure.[3] The ease with which roads could be closed or diverted by estate owners is shown in the case of Joseph Damer, Lord Milton of Milton Abbas, who applied to the Dorset Quarter Sessions in 1763 for permission to close three roads which passed close to his house. A commission of a dozen leading gentlemen, 'honest and lawful men of the County', was appointed to inquire into the matter. However, since all were friends or neighbours of Lord Milton, not surprisingly, they reported that

It will be of no damage or prejudice either to our said Lord the King or to any other or to Passengers and Travellers passing to and from the said Parishes of Milton Abbas, Winterborne Stickland and Stoke Wake or to and from any other Parishes or Places, for that there are other roads or highways near the said roads or highways to be inclosed . . .

All other roads were, in fact, at some distance, and the modern traveller still has to make a detour of more than 3km (2 miles) around the estate.[4]

By the mid-nineteenth century such inconvenient road diversions were not so calmly accepted, and an indication of this is to be found only a few miles from Milton Abbas. At Charborough the main road from Dorchester to Wimborne makes a considerable detour around the Erle Drax estate at Charborough Park, and an inscription on the lodge and gateway which now block the previous route records that the new road was 'projected and completed through the instrumentality of J.S.W. Sawbridge Erle Drax Esq., M.P. in the years 1841 and 1842'. Another inscription on the same gateway, however, records that the diversion had not gone unchallenged.

This Road through the Park was closed by order of the Magistrates which was appealed against by James John Farquharson Esq. at the Epiphany Quarter Sessions held at Dorchester January 4th 1841 and after a trial of three days the order was confirmed by the order of Twelve Honest Jurymen.

At Milton Abbas the closure of the roads close to his house by Lord Milton during the 1760s was soon followed by the rebuilding of his mansion and the removal of the small town which was situated near his house. This illustrates both the power of eighteenth-century landlords and its limitations, for although Lord Milton, who later became Earl of Dorchester, was able to remove the town which possessed a grammar school, six public houses, weekly markets and annual fairs, yet he was obliged to wait until tenants died or he was able to

**49** *Wentworth Castle (Yorkshire). Eighteenth-century lodge built to resemble a church at the castle entrance. to the castle. (D. Hey.)*

secure the lease of their property, and the whole process took him nearly 20 years (1771–90). In place of the town he laid out an elegant park and lake to designs by Capability Brown, surrounding it by a park wall 9km (5½ miles) in length.

For household servants and some of the other inhabitants removed from the town, the model village of Milton Abbas was designed by Sir William Chambers half a mile away and out of sight of the mansion. The new village, with its church and almshouses provided by Lord Dorchester, remains as one of the most attractive of all

such creations, although only a small proportion of those displaced from the former town could have been accommodated in it. When Sir Frederick Morton Eden visited Dorset during the 1790s to collect material for his survey of the *State of the Poor* (published in 1797) he was not only appalled by the low wages and poor conditions of labourers in the county, but also reported that

. . . what is more singular the town of Abbey Milton, which was formerly the central market of the county, is now a fish-pond . . .[5]

## Model villages

There are many similar examples of new villages built during the eighteenth century to rehouse those who were displaced by the creation of parks or in order to create an appropriate setting for a newly built or enlarged mansion. One of the best is Nuneham Courtenay (Oxfordshire) where Lord Harcourt laid out the new village of formal cottages along the main Oxford to Henley road during the 1760s to rehouse the villagers displaced by his demolition of the old village which had been close to his mansion. An early model village is New Houghton (Norfolk), a single street of 24 solidly-built, very plain houses and 8 almshouses, constructed in 1729 for the Prime Minister, Sir Robert Walpole, to replace the original village which was situated within the recently enlarged park. Only the parish church survives in the park to mark the original village, while the new village stands at the park entrance.

At Harewood (Yorkshire) the village and surrounding estate were acquired during the late seventeenth century by Henry Lascelles, who had made a fortune as a director of the East India Company, through the ribbon trade and as a collector of customs in Barbados. His son, Edwin Lascelles, inherited the property in 1759 and immediately set about altering it out of all recognition. The village was removed to make way for a new mansion designed by John Carr of York and decorated by Robert Adam with furniture by Thomas Chippendale, while the 810ha (2000 acres) of parkland were landscaped by Capability Brown. Only the medieval church remained, with its remarkable collection of monuments, including six medieval tomb-chests of alabaster. The new village, also designed by John Carr, was laid out beyond the lodges at the gates to the park, the robust terraces providing an impressive approach to the mansion. Similar villages were created

at Euston (Suffolk), Kedleston (Derbyshire) and at Bowood (Wiltshire) where the village of Sandy Lane was built to rehouse those whose houses were swept away when Capability Brown remodelled the park and created a lake by the house. One of the most interesting of such estate villages is Edensor (Derbyshire) created during the early nineteenth century by the sixth Duke of Devonshire across the valley from Chatsworth but out of sight of the house.

The cottages at Edensor are well built in local stone with large gardens (Fig. 50). The plans and architecture have obviously been culled from several different journals and pattern books, and they range from Gothic, Renaissance and Tudor to Georgian, Italianate and Swiss 'chalet' styles. The large church was added during the 1860s to a Gothic design by Sir Gilbert Scott. The whole effect is self-consciously picturesque and romantic, although no doubt the cottages are much better built and spacious than those on the earlier site which they replaced. Describing the cottages at Edensor, a local directory of 1840 declared that 'Everything tends to show his Grace's taste, good feeling and liberal disposition towards those in humbled circumstances'.

At Harlaxton (Lincolnshire), where an extravagantly grand mansion was designed for Gregory Gregory by Anthony Salvin and built during the 1830s, the village was also totally reconstructed. Advice was sought from John Claudius Loudon, whose extensive writings on estate cottages had become so influential, and the result was a remarkable variety of styles, decoration and picturesque details such as elaborate chimneys, dormer windows, decorative tiles, balconies, porches and curious garden ornaments.

Thomas Anson, the owner of Shugborough near Stafford enlarged the park and in the process destroyed most of the former village. He also employed James Stuart, who became known as 'Athenian'

*Edensor (Derbyshire). One of the Chatsworth estate houses in the village of c.1839.*

Stuart from his liking for neo-Greek architecture, to adorn the park with a Grecian temple, an 'Arch of Hadrian', a Lantern of Diogenes and a Tower of the Winds, and also commissioned a Chinese pavilion or summer house and bridge, a mock-medieval ruin, a large monument to a cat and other garden features. The mansion at Shugborough was also enlarged and a vast new stable block and estate workshops were created. Thomas Anson also built a notable model farm there which will be discussed later in the chapter. The money which made all this possible came from his brother, Admiral George Anson, whose celebrated voyage around the world during the years 1740–44 in the *Centurion*, and capture of a Spanish galleon and its treasure brought him great wealth amounting to some £800,000, a sum worth more than £50 million in late twentieth-century terms, of which the Admiral's share was three eighths. It was therefore particularly appropriate that a Tower of the Winds should be created near the mansion in honour of the motive force that had propelled his ship.

Admiral Lord Anson also purchased Moor Park, the largest house in Hertfordshire and spent £80 000 between 1755 and 1760 on landscaping the grounds to the designs of Capability Brown. This also included a Temple of the Winds which prompted Dr Johnson's comment

A grateful mind I praise! All to the winds he
    owed
And so upon the Winds a Temple he bestowed.[6]

**51** *Great Tew (Oxfordshire). Cottages in the attractive estate village.*

In all parts of the country during the eighteenth century villages, hamlets, farms and arable lands were swept away in the quest for privacy and the desire to create a setting appropriate to the rank and power of estate owners. At Normanton (Rutland) the medieval church and its village were both destroyed by Sir Gilbert Heathcote; a new village was created elsewhere and a new church was built during the 1820s to form a feature within the extended park. The grounds of Wimpole Hall were transformed by Capability Brown between 1767 and 1773, and were later altered again by Humphry Repton. The village was removed and replaced by a small group of cottages grouped with suitable humility around the park gates, while the medieval church was rebuilt and allowed to remain as a feature of the parkland, along with a sham castle and other 'eye-catchers' designed to be seen from the house.[7]

At Escrick (Yorkshire) the Thompson family secured an Act of Parliament in 1781 which enabled them to enclose the open fields, replace the village, divert the roads away from their manor house and rebuild the church. The house was enlarged with an elegant new front, large stable block and kennels while the grounds were landscaped and included a lake, duck decoys, planned woodland and a temple.[8] At Clumber the Duke of Newcastle's great house of *c.*1770 (now demolished) and landscaped park, woodlands and lake were also graced with a fine church erected by the seventh Duke during the 1880s at a cost of £30,000. The church remains in the elegant parkland as a monument to the wealth and power of such noble families.

By the mid-nineteenth century many parks had been extended and covered huge acreages. The park at Holkham was 3000 acres and included a large lake and belts of sheltering woodland; Woburn (Bedfordshire) contained 2400 acres and was 19km (12 miles) in circumference.

Central Nottinghamshire possessed a group of large parks, including Clumber, Thoresby, Welbeck and Rufford, in an area known as the 'dukeries'. The wealth concentrated in these estates was immense, and at Thoresby, for example, during the 1860s and 1870s Earl Manvers spent nearly £200,000 of income from his vast estates and collieries on a new mansion, stables,

gardens, parkland, estate cottages and a new church for his tenants and servants in the adjoining village of Perlethorpe. The park at Blenheim contains 2700 acres, and is 15km (9 miles) in circumference.

The model village estate cottages, built by landowners, were far better, more comfortable and healthier than the insanitary hovels which they so frequently replaced. However, occupants of the new dwellings were compelled to remain on the estate, and both they and their families were totally dependent upon the landowner, both for employment and for accommodation. Equally, those who were provided with allotments or potato ground were unlikely to look for other employment during the summer and autumn, when their labour was most needed on the estate and when alternative and better-paid work was most

**52** *Eastnor (Hereforshire). Cottages of c.1850 at the gates of Eastnor Castle.*

readily obtainable elsewhere. In the creation of model villages or the rebuilding of labourers' cottages on their estates, the motives of landowners ranged from a benevolent desire to see their workers well–housed and contented, to a concern that an attractive village with picturesque cottages and suitably subservient tenants should, like elegant lodges, grand entrance gates or long driveways complete with avenues of trees, add dignity to the approach to their mansion, as well as providing evidence of the social concern of the owner.[9]

The picturesque and romantic effect of some model villages, and especially of the almshouses provided for elderly retainers and former servants, was further enhanced by the requirement that the inhabitants should wear distinctive clothing. Thus at Milton Abbas the almswomen had to wear pointed hats, at Old Warden (Bedfordshire) the cottagers were ordered to wear red clothing; and at Selworthy (Somerset) the women were encouraged to gather under

**53** *Blaise Castle hamlet, near Bristol. The hamlet consists of ten cottages, irregularly arranged around a small green; it was designed by John Nash in 1811 for the Quaker banker, J.S. Harford, and was intended as a model village for elderly and deserving persons. All the cottages are different and self-consciously romantic and picturesque.*

the walnut trees on the village green wearing their distinctive red capes to provide an idyllic picture of pastoral charm and contentment; the capes were supplied by Lady Acland, wife of the founder of the model village, Sir Thomas Dyke Acland.

The successful running of a great household, with its multitude of indoor servants, as well as those required for the gardens, stables, workshops and home farm, required a large labour force. It was convenient that the labourers should live reasonably close at hand, especially in view of the very long hours of work, and yet that their families should not intrude upon the peace and privacy of the landowner. Early model villages such as Nuneham Courtenay, New Houghton or Harewood were purely practical and arranged on either side of a road. The consciously 'picturesque' and romantic style of model villages achieved great popularity following the fame of Blaise Castle hamlet, on the outskirts of Bristol (Fig. 53). The Quaker banker and estate owner, John Harford, employed John Nash to design a little group of cottages grouped around a village green, as 'retreats for aged persons, who had moved in respectable walks of life, but had fallen under misfortunes, preserving little or nothing, in the shock of adversity but unblemished character'. Each cottage is different, with high-pitched roofs, highly-decorated chimneys, dovecots, elaborate gables, dormer windows and porches, and the whole hamlet represents an attempt to create a romantic vision of the past. They were built in 1810–11 and rapidly achieved great fame. An early visitor remarked that 'the smiling village' added greatly to the attraction of the estate and also 'forms a memorial of the founder's exemplary benevolence'.[10] Blaise Hamlet inspired many other essays in the creation of picturesque villages or of *cottages ornées*, among them Sandy Lane on the Bowood estate, Selworthy (Somerset), Somerleyton

(Suffolk), Ilam (Derbyshire), Old Warden (Bedfordshire) or Great Badminton (Gloucestershire). It is significant that the Duke of Devonshire visited Blaise Castle hamlet shortly before work began on his romantic model village at Edensor.

An even earlier example of a picturesque model village was created at Erlestoke (Wiltshire) where the landowner, Josiah Smith, built a mansion and laid out an elaborate park during the 1780s. He also rebuilt the village with the cottages neatly spaced out on either side of the road, many of them containing architectural and sculptured fragments from an earlier mansion. The whole village provided a romantic and attractive approach to the mansion, and obviously impressed William Cobbett, who saw it during the 1820s:

I came to a hamlet called Earl's Stoke, the houses of which stand at a few yards from each other, on the two sides of the road; every house is white; and the front of every one is covered with some sort of clematis, or with rose-trees or jasmines. It was easy to guess that the whole belonged to one owner . . .[11]

## Housing conditions

While many of the cottages provided in these estate villages are undoubtedly picturesque, they were not designed primarily for the convenience of the occupants, and many are small, the rooms are low, while the thatched roofs, which were considered essential for a true romantic appearance, overhung the small leaded windows so that the interiors were very dark. But they were superior to the cottages and hovels lived in by many labourers. In the south-west of England during the eighteenth and early nineteenth centuries the farm labourers not only had extremely low wages and appalling conditions, but were abominably housed. In 1795 Thomas Davis, who was steward to the Marquess of Bath at

Longleat, commented that

Humanity shudders at the idea of the industrious
labourer, with a wife and five or six children,
being obliged to live, or rather exist, in a
wretched, damp, gloomy room of 10 or 12 feet
square, and that room without a floor; but
common decency must revolt at considering that
over the wretched apartment there is only one
chamber, to hold all the miserable beds of the
miserable inhabitants.[12]

In 1826 William Cobbett rode along the
valley of the Salisbury Avon and wrote that

In taking my leave of this beautiful vale, I have to
express my deep shame as an Englishman, at
beholding the general extreme poverty of those
who cause this vale to produce such quantities of
food and raiment. This is, I verily believe it, the
worst used labouring people upon the face of this
earth. Dogs and hogs and horses are treated with
more civility; and as to food and lodging, how
gladly would the labourers change with them.[13]

Of the labourers' hovels in Northumberland
in 1851 Sir James Caird, a sober and
detached observer, wrote that they were
worse than 'in some of the most wretched
villages in Ireland'.

In 1867 a parliamentary commission was
appointed to enquire into the 'Employment
of Children, Young Persons and Women in
Agriculture'. This produced a mass of
evidence about the domestic and daily life of
working people, and their housing
conditions. For example, one of the
commissioners, the Hon. E. Stanhope,
reported of Dorset that

the cottages of this county are more ruinous and
contain worse accommodation than those of any
other county I have visited, except Shropshire
. . . The estate of Lord Rivers . . . is notorious
for its bad cottages. And such villages as Bere
Regis, Fordington, Winfrith, Cranborne or
Charminster (in which there is an average of 7
persons to a house) are a disgrace to the owners
of land, and contain many cottages unfit for
human habitation.[14]

Eighteen years later in 1885 the *Report of the
Royal Commission of the Housing of the
Working Class* showed that conditions on
many estates had improved very little.[15] The
mid-nineteenth century surveyor and land-
agent, William Sturge, who was as familiar
with the slums of Bristol as with the villages
of north Somerset, was in no doubt that
conditions in the villages were often worse
than those in the towns because of the bad
drainage, overcrowding and general filth
and declared that 'A country village is in
consequence often far more unhealthy than
the town'.

Similar appalling standards of housing
were to be found in rural areas all over the
country, and as late as 1900 in an article on
Lord Wantage's estate in Berkshire, *The
Rural World* commented that

. . . one may travel village after village and find
numerous specimens of dwellings which, to say
the least, are most undesirable. Broken-down
old cottages, consisting of one room downstairs,
and one or two upstairs, cannot be fit places in
which to rear a family morally and physically
healthy . . . The worst cottages are commonly
those owned by small owners or speculators . . .
their main if not only object being the receipt of
as much rent as they can exact. Where, however,
a large landowner owns the whole or practically
the whole of a village, then you will find cottages
good both as to quality and size . . .

The writer went on to praise the cottages
provided by Lord Wantage on his Berkshire
estate villages of Ardington and Lockinge.
Each pair of cottages cost £390–400 to
build, and provided good accommodation
together with gardens and pig sties. With
rents of no more than 1s 0d or 1s 6d per
week however, the writer admitted that
'The rent charged by no means represents a
commercial percentage on the capital
outlay'.[16]

A lead had been given to philanthropic
estate owners by Prince Albert who rebuilt
many of the cottages on the royal estates,

**54**   *Preston-on-Stour (Warwickshire). Mid-nineteenth-century estate cottages.*

and his example was quickly followed by others. The production of plans for improved but cheaply-erected labourers' cottages became the general hobby of both professional and amateur architects and innumerable ideas and proposals were published (Fig. 54).

One of the earliest advocates of improved housing was Nathaniel Kent, who acted as land agent and adviser to numerous estates and whose book *Hints to Gentlemen of Landed Property*, published in 1775, was widely read. This included detailed plans and suggestions for improved cottages, and Kent wrote that

I think it as necessary to provide plain and comfortable habitations for the Poor as it is to provide comfortable and convenient dwellings for cattle . . .

He also pointed out that those living in the improved cottages would be 'permanently fixed to the soil' and be less likely to cause trouble or join in 'occasional Tumults'.[17] In 1832 John Claudius Loudon produced his influential book, *Encyclopaedia of Cottage, Farm and Villa Architecture*, with 1138 closely-printed pages and many plans; and the pages of periodicals such as the *Builder* and the *Journal of the Royal Agricultural Society of England* contained many plans, descriptions and discussions of model cottages. Societies were founded to encourage landowners such as 'The Central Cottage Improvement Society', and 'The Society for Improving the Condition of the Labouring Classes' of which Prince Albert became patron in 1848.

The provision of improved housing for

**55**   *Castle Howard (Yorkshire). Entrance lodge of 1874 to the Castle Howard estate.*

labourers was not cheap, and many benevolent landlords were embarrassed by the state of some of the cottages on their estates. When the philanthropist seventh Earl of Shaftesbury succeeded to his estate at Wimborne St Giles (Dorset) on the death of his father in 1851, he found the accounts in chaos, a mass of debts and the farms and cottages in a deplorable condition. In despair at the situation he wrote

Alas, alas, I am powerless; I can neither build cottages nor dismiss the farmer from his land without money to fall back upon.

He also deplored the fact that although he had been so outspoken in his condemnation of the bad housing in industrial towns and had so strongly stressed the influence of dwellings on the habits and character of

labourers, he had inherited a large estate with appalling housing conditions.

I have passed my life in rating others for allowing rotten houses and immoral, unhealthy dwellings; and now I come into an estate rife with abominations! Why, there are things here to make one's flesh creep; and I have not a farthing to set them right.

By great efforts, including the sale of land and plate, Lord Shaftesbury was able to transform the estate, and by 1885, the year of his death, his agent could report to the Royal Commission on the Housing of the Working Class that 'of 537 cottages on the estate, 12 were "bad", 77 were in "fair repair" and the rest were "excellent" '. Most of the cottages had three bedrooms, and the rents ranged from £1 to £3 per annum.[18]

The interest of landowners in cottage improvement is evident from the numerous schemes, proposals, collections of plans, pattern books and specifications culled from books and journals and from correspondence on the subject with other estate owners which are to be found in numerous estate records. For example, the records of the Earls of Pembroke, whose vast estates were centred upon Wilton, include many cottage plans and proposals for improvements to farms and other estate buildings, and the surviving buildings show that many of the schemes were carried out. Likewise, Sir Greville Smyth at Ashton Court, near Bristol, collected numerous examples of cottage plans from landowners all over the country, as well as from his near neighbours, and large numbers of substantial and roomy labourers' dwellings were built on the estate during the last decades of the nineteenth century. The Smyth family also built almshouses and a school in the village, as well as a house for the village policeman, complete with a cell.

Large numbers of cottages were built on the estate of Lord Grey at Howick (Northumberland), and the seventh Duke of Bedford was responsible for building 288 cottages on his Devonshire estates and 374 on his estates in Bedfordshire.[19] The first Duke of Westminster, a romantic idealist and practical philanthropist, built 48 farmhouses, 360 cottages, 8 schools, 7 village halls and 3 churches on his Cheshire estates centred on Eaton Hall, including the

**56** *Sherborne (Gloucestershire). Early nineteenth-century estate cottage, incorporating a doorway from the demolished twelfth-century parish church.*

notable labourers' cottages at Aldford, one of the largest of all estate villages; while at Peckforton (Cheshire) Lord Tollemache spent over £280,000 on farm houses and new cottages.[20] Lord Yarborough's estate at Brocklesby (Lincolnshire) comprised 55,000 acres spread across the Lincolnshire Wolds, and during the mid-nineteenth century numerous brick-built cottages were erected, each bearing the family coat of arms, and giving a distinctive appearance to the villages on the estate. The characteristic yellow bricks were produced on the estate and were used for farms, barns, farm buildings and schools, as well as for labourers' cottages, and continue to provide a clear indication of the profound influence of a great estate upon the landscape (Fig. 57).[21]

On the Coke estates at Holkham large numbers of labourers' cottages were built during the nineteenth century, at first in the village at the gates of the hall, but later throughout the estate. At Lockinge and Ardington from 1858 the estate farms and cottages were improved by Major Robert James Lindsay, later Lord Wantage, who rebuilt many of the farms, barns and cottages throughout the estate, and created a model village at Lockinge. Like many other estate owners, Lord Wantage used his own workmen for the building work, and established an estate yard, employing more than 100 men, with carpenters, bricklayers, blacksmiths and farriers, using steam-driven machinery.[22]

The extensive use of published pattern books or plans and the number of competitions for cottage designs organized and published by journals, means that

**57**   *Brocklesby (Lincolnshire). Elegant workers' cottages on the estate of the Earl of Yarborough.*

cottages of a similar style and with the same decorative features such as elaborate barge boards, stone mouldings, steeply-pitched roofs, dormer windows, ornate chimneys and rustic porches are encountered all over the country. Often they are distinguished only by the estate arms, initials or characteristic motif.

Only landlords who were benevolently inclined or socially concerned would indulge in the building or improvement of labourers' cottages, since the return which could be expected was much less than would have been received if the money was invested elsewhere. Brick and tile cottages such as those built by Thomas Coke, Earl of Leicester, on his estate at Holkham in 1819 would have cost £110–115 each, but the rents were no more than £3 3s 0d a year.

A pair of cottages built for Sir Arthur Elton at Clevedon (Somerset) in 1860 cost £247 12s 6d to build, but the annual rental was no more than £2 2s 0d. By the end of the nineteenth century well-built cottages on Lord Wantage's estate in Berkshire, which had cost £390–400 the pair to build, were still only producing £3 15s 0d a year in rent.

Improved cottages and model villages were not only built by benevolent landowners during the nineteenth century, but were also erected by philanthropic or politically-motivated societies and by industrialists aiming to provide better housing for their workers. Among the most notable societies were the Chartists, who campaigned for political reform but also established several rural settlements with small-holdings, notably at Charterville

**58** *Snigs End, Corse (Gloucestershire). One of the houses on the Chartist settlement, which was founded by Feargus O'Connor in 1847–8.*

**59**  *Snigs End, Corse. Former Chartist school of 1847–8, now the Prince of Wales inn.*

(Oxfordshire), Great Dodford (Worcestershire) and at Snigs End (Figs 58 and 59) and Lowbands (Gloucestershire). Villages created by industrialists include Somerleyton (Suffolk) built during the 1840s by Sir Morton Peto, who had become extremely wealthy as a building and railway contractor; the village contains 28 consciously picturesque cottages with thatched roofs and elaborate chimneys and also a school, all grouped around a village green. Other examples are Titus Salt's village at Saltaire near Bradford; Cadbury's model village settlement at Bournville on the outskirts of Birmingham; New Earswick (Yorkshire); and the attractive village created by I.K. Brunel for the workers on the Great Western Railway at Swindon. In addition there were, of course, countless smaller schemes undertaken by benevolent employers.[20]

## Model farms and improved farm buildings

Throughout the country estate landscapes are also characterized by the solidly-built farm buildings erected during the 'high-farming' era of Victorian England. The farm houses are well-built and spacious, designed to attract the best tenants, while estate farm buildings are generally stone or brick-built with large barns, good cattle housing and convenient dairies. The distinctive styles adopted by each estate are often apparent, and many have coats of arms or other distinguishing features. For example, in Northamptonshire the farms rebuilt during the nineteenth century on the Spencer estates around Althorp or the Grafton estates surrounding the mansion at Pottersbury are easily recognizable. Likewise, around the Duke of Westminster's Grosvenor estate in

Cheshire, the Portman estates in Dorset, the Pembroke estates in south Wiltshire or the Marlborough's widespread lands in Oxfordshire and on the territories of countless other landowners, the fine nineteenth-century farm buildings provide eloquent testimony to the agricultural prosperity of mid-Victorian England.[24]

In order to set an example of the best farming practice and of improved methods to their tenants, and in the hope that higher yields would eventually produce increased rents, many landlords also established model or 'example' farms (Fig. 60). Such farms were described by the agricultural writer, William Marshall, as 'a seminary of improvements for the benefit and advancement of the estate at large'.

Model-farm buildings incorporated all the latest ideas and technological innovations of the age, notably in the provision of power through the horse engine or 'gin', and later by the steam engine. The buildings were carefully planned for maximum efficiency and productivity, while the land was used in such a way as to demonstrate modern techniques, alongside the use of new varieties of crops, new implements and

**60** *Duke of Marlborough's estate (Oxfordshire). Early nineteenth-century farmstead and farmhouse. (Rural History Centre, University of Reading.)*

**61**  *Model farmstead, Steeple Ashton (Wiltshire). Photographed from the tower of the nearby parish church, this farmstead shows many of the innovations which have been adopted by farmers during the past century and a half.*

improved breeds of sheep and cattle (Fig. 61).

A farm which exercised a profound influence during the early nineteenth century was Coke's Park Farm at Holkham where the annual sheep-shearings became an important means of spreading new farming knowledge. Likewise, the Duke of Bedford held similar gatherings at Woburn, where the earliest steam-driven threshing machine was installed in 1804. An ardent agriculturalist, George III established the Norfolk Farm at Windsor during the late eighteenth century, and this was rebuilt during the 1850s by Prince Albert, who also added two more showpieces in Windsor Great Park: the royal dairy at Frogmore,

beautifully tiled and equipped throughout; and the Flemish Farm built of brick with extensive cattle sheds to house the royal herd of champion Herefords.

A model and experimental farm also formed part of the Royal College of Agriculture which was established at Cirencester in 1845, through the influence of the local gentry, most notably Earl Bathurst, on whose estate the college was situated (Fig. 62). At Shugborough, a notable range of farm buildings was designed by Samuel Wyatt for Lord Anson early in the nineteenth century, providing well-built barns with water-powered equipment, store houses, workshops, labourers' accommodation, stables, cattle

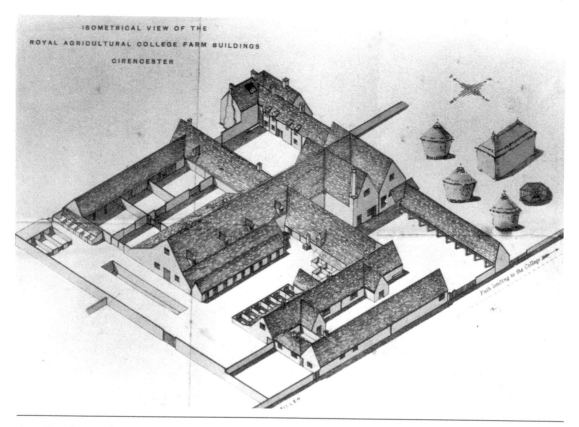

ISOMETRICAL VIEW OF THE
ROYAL AGRICULTURAL COLLEGE FARM BUILDINGS
CIRENCESTER

**62** *Royal Agricultural College, Cirencester (Wiltshire). Buildings erected in c.1860 for the College which had been founded in 1845. (Celia Miller.)*

sheds, a mill and a poultry house. Even the Tower of the Winds, built at Shugborough in 1765 was converted into a model dairy.[25]

At Sandwell in south Staffordshire, the Earl of Dartmouth erected a fine model farm early in the eighteenth century, built in brick and incorporating all the latest farming ideas for cattle housing, dairy farming and the storage and processing of arable crops. This farm has recently been restored by Sandwell Borough Council and is open to the public. The model farm built by Baron Hawke, son of the naval hero Admiral Lord Hawke, on his estate at Scarthingwell (Yorkshire) during the 1780s greatly impressed the authors of the *General View of the Agriculture of the West Riding of Yorkshire*, who visited it in 1793 and described it as follows:

Here we beg leave to notice the suite of farm offices lately erected by the Right Honourable Lord Hawke, which affords an elegant pattern for his neighbours. His Lordship has built for his own use a large farmyard, conveniently formed and situated, with a threshing machine, a mill for grinding rape cake, stables for 25 horses and 32 oxen, besides cowsheds etc. divided into four yards, two of which have ponds, besides the pumps. The stables for the horses are placed on the East and West sides of the farmyard, which is free from buildings on the South, and sheltered on the North by the barn and oxhouses, which separate it from the principal stackyard. This yard is divided from the two others by open hay barns, tiled with slate eaves and with chimnies also of brick to let out the steam. The average of the boarded granaries amounts in length to 160

**63** *Eastwood Manor farm, East Harptree, near Bristol. This model farm, containing 0.5ha (1¼ acres) under one roof, was built in 1859 as the centre of a 900 acre farm. Within, everything from cattle-housing to threshing equipment and grain storage was provided according to the most up-to-date methods of the time.*

feet, and in bredth to 21 feet. There are trap doors in them to let down the corn, when sacked, into waggons which may be loaded and locked up at the same time. The corn in the yard is stacked on wooden frames placed on stone pillars and caps. When we saw it, Lord Hawke proposed to make further improvements on it, and to build a house for his steward. The whole indeed forms a complete, elegant and convenient suite of farm offices, covering from one to two

acres of ground, and is in every respect becoming a nobleman who justly considers the cultivation of the earth as the most useful and necessary of human employments.

In Essex John Joseph Mechi, who had made a fortune from his Magic Razor Strops and from patent gas lamps, purchased an estate at Tiptree Hall and during the 1840s, with enormous energy and enthusiasm, set up a

**64**   *Whitfield Example Farm, Falfield (Gloucestershire). Built during the 1840s on the estate of the Earl Ducie and designed by his agent John Morton, a leading exponent of agricultural improvements. (Colin Miller.)*

model farm using all the latest techniques and erecting lavish buildings, regardless of expense.[26] On a more modest scale the Revd Archdeacon Anthony Huxtable of Sutton Waldron on the chalklands of Dorset provided a model farm in order to give an example of the best and most modern farming methods to his parishioners. In north-west Berkshire a famous experimental farm was set up by the agricultural pioneer and member of Parliament, Philip Pusey. He inherited an estate of 5000 acres at Pusey in 1830, and became one of the most influential advocates of improved farming, a founder-member of the Royal Agricultural Society in 1838, editor of its important journal, and the man responsible for the agricultural implement section of the Great Exhibition in 1851.

An excellent example of a model farm survives at East Harptree (Somerset), south of Bristol (Fig. 63). The farmstead, which was built in 1859, contains 0.5ha (1¼ acres) under a single roof, with cast-iron pillars and extensive use of glass and galvanized iron. Within, everything from cattle housing to grain storage is provided, and power was originally provided throughout the building by a water-wheel and a complex system of shafts and belts. The stream which drove the water-wheel could be diverted to sluice out the cattle pens, and the resulting slurry was stored in large tanks before being pumped out to the fields. This model farmstead was at the centre of a 900 acre farm, and was designed by Robert Smith, who had previously worked for Prince Albert on the layout of the Windsor farms.[27]

The ideas and hopes which motivated

# 7 Philanthropy, industry and adaptation to change

The owners of major estates made an impact upon the landscape of towns and villages throughout the country by the endowment and building of almshouses, hospitals, schools, meeting rooms, market houses and town halls, as well as by the reconstruction or restoration of churches. This long-established tradition of philanthropy was to reach its height during the nineteenth century under the impetus of Victorian piety and public spirit, when it was not uncommon for between 5 and 10 per cent of the gross income of landed estates to be paid out in charities of all kinds.[1]

Many landowners provided schools on their estates, and during the decade before 1870 there was a rush to build schools which could be closely controlled by the landowner and supervised by the Church of England rather than have a Board school provided under the Act of 1870 with democratic control and non-sectarian education. At Holkham, Thomas Coke, who was concerned with every aspect of life on his estate provided a village school in 1822 which was administered by the estate office. The Duke of Marlborough provided or contributed towards schools in many of the villages on his estate; at Cassington he gave the site for a school and schoolmaster's house, placing the administration under the control of his private chaplain because of the indifference of the incumbent. At Ashover (Derbyshire) the Nodder family, who were for several generations both squires and

parsons, provided a school in 1845 with the inscription over the door 'Bring up the child in the way he should go'.

All over the country schools were founded (Fig. 67) or largely funded by gentry families in association with the Church of England and through its splendidly-named society *The National Society for Promoting the Education of the Poor in the Principles of the Established Church*. Such schools have the words 'National School' above the doorway, and a remarkable number have dates in the mid-nineteenth century, as landowners and clergy alike rushed to found schools before Parliament moved to fill the gaps that remained with non-denominational 'Board Schools', or before schools could be built by the nonconformist society the 'British and Foreign Schools Society', whose schools bore the inscription 'British School'. At Baldersby (Yorkshire) Viscount Downe provided a church, vicarage, numerous brick cottages and a school for his tenants during the 1850s; at Goodwood (Sussex) there was an estate nurse, pensions for retired workers, clubs and societies for the tenants and schools in the surrounding villages, all provided by the Duke of Richmond. The Duke of Beaufort's almshouses of *c.* 1714, with his arms prominently displayed on all three gables, dwarf the other houses in the model village which is clustered around the gates of the great mansion at Badminton. The accounts

**67** *Preston-on-Stour (Warwickshire). School of 1848 on the Alscot Park estate.*

of Lord Pembroke's estates in Wiltshire show an increasing amount spent on charities and education during the mid-nineteenth century, and out of the 30 parishes in which his Lordship possessed property, nine already had satisfactory schools, in four others the site and school building were provided by the estate and for nine others substantial contributions were made towards the costs.[2]

At the villages of Arley and Great Bedworth (Cheshire) during the 1860s the landowner, Rowland Egerton-Warburton of Arley Hall, provided a new church, a school, a post-office and shop for his tenants, as well as rebuilding many of the cottages, including on them prominent mottoes such as the stark warning 'No labour, no bread', or the gentler

> Take thy calling Thankfullie
> Love thy neighbour Neighbourlie
> Shun the path to Beggarie

## 'Open' and 'closed' villages

Such villages, where the dominance of a single landowner was supreme, contrasted strongly with the much more numerous 'open' villages, where there were several landowners or a large number of freeholders, and these distinctions are often still very apparent. 'Open' villages tended to be more populous, since settlement was not strictly controlled. Unplanned, haphazardly arranged and cheaply-built cottages and hovels proliferated, no distinctive building style was imposed, nonconformist chapels could be established without interference, and public houses and beer shops could proliferate.

In estate or 'closed' villages settlement and building were tightly controlled by the landowner, high standards and uniform styles of architecture were maintained. The influence, initials and coat of arms of the landowner are likely to be visible, nonconformists were probably discouraged, since tenants were expected to attend church and to worship under the watchful gaze of the landowner in his family pew, while if a public house was permitted at all, it will bear the name and arms of the landowner.

Among the multitude of such 'closed' villages all over the country, a good example where the dominance of a single landowner is still very obvious, is Belton near Grantham (Lincolnshire). For several centuries the Brownlow family presided over the village and during the late seventeenth century had rebuilt their mansion, Belton House, on the grandest scale, producing what Sir Nikolaus Pevsner described as 'perhaps the most satisfying among the later 17th century houses in England'. Later the house was enlarged, and provided with entrance gates, lodges, large stables and a landscaped park, complete with temple, obelisk, Gothic ruin and other furnishings in the approved fashion, and including the parish church, filled with the sumptuous memorials to members of the family. During the early nineteenth century the cottages in the village were rebuilt in a Tudor style, creating a notable 'model village', while the Brownlow family founded almshouses in 1827 (Fig. 68) and provided a village cross, smithy and elegant pump for the convenience of their tenants.

The Earl was patron of the living, and since the rector was frequently a relative, the rectory house was also rebuilt to provide a large and suitable residence. The Brownlows also paid for the thorough restoration of the parish church, unfortunately removing many of its medieval features in the process, but providing a well-built structure to house all the family monuments which are crowded

**68**   *Belton (Lincolnshire). Almshouses, founded in 1827 by the Cust family. From their large and elegant mansion beside the parish church the family exercised a benevolent despotism over this excellent example of an estate village.*

within it. Until the later nineteenth century there was no nonconformist chapel in the village, and the tenants, household servants and estate workers were obviously expected to attend church on Sundays. In 1851, out of the 182 inhabitants of the village, 135 (74 per cent) attended the services in the parish church.

## Towns and estates

Towns also benefited from the philanthropy or enterprise of nearby estate owners. The town hall at Woodstock (Oxfordshire) was given to the town by the fourth Duke of Marlborough in 1766 and his arms are prominently displayed upon it; he also provided a water-supply and a fire service for the town and had trees planted to beautify the streets. At Alnwick the large market house, Northumberland Hall, was provided for the town at the expense of the Duke of Northumberland in 1826. The market cross at Swaffham (Norfolk), which is a large open rotunda situated in the market place and surmounted by the figure of Ceres, was erected by the Earl of Orford in 1783. At Chippenham (Wiltshire) the town hall was built in 1848 at the expense of the wealthy landowner, Joseph Neeld, whose estate was nearby and who was MP for the borough. At Warminster (Wiltshire), which is close to the Longleat estate, Lord Bath provided the town hall in 1855 at a cost of £1500, and two years later built the grandly-named Athenaeum in order that 'the middle and lower classes' might pursue 'refined and intellectual pleasures'.

Bath developed into the premier spa and resort in England during the eighteenth century under the patronage of several leading landowners, notably the Duke of Chandos; while Buxton owed its popularity as a spa to the Dukes of Devonshire. The second Duke commissioned John Baker of Rowsley to reconstruct the baths during the early eighteenth century, and during the 1780s the fifth Duke employed John Carr of York, the most celebrated architect in the north of England, to design and build a crescent of houses for visitors to the spa at a cost of some £12,000. The Marquess of Hastings attempted to develop Ashby de la Zouch (Leicestershire) as a spa, building the Ivanhoe Baths in 1822 and the Hastings Hotel in 1826.

## Churches and church restorations

Most notable of all was the rebuilding or drastic restoration of churches, often accompanied by the erection of huge monuments to the landowner's family (Fig. 69) or by the building of a separate mausoleum. On the Sledmere estate (Yorkshire) no less than 12 churches were built or rebuilt by Sir Tatton Sykes during the period 1863–79, and another eight were restored. In all parts of the country the number of new churches was amazing, and estate owners were in the forefront of the contributors to the building. During the period 1845–69 there were 106 new churches built in the diocese of Oxford; in the same period 110 new churches were consecrated in the diocese of Manchester. Between 1832 and 1864 there were 82 new churches built in Hampshire, and 87 in Surrey. One third of all the Church of England churches in Staffordshire in 1851 had been built since 1800, 82 of them since 1843.

One example out of the many individuals who contributed so generously to church building and restoration was Mary Caroline, Marchioness of Ailesbury, who lived at Tottenham House in Savernake Forest (Wiltshire) from 1837 to 1879. During that time she was responsible for the rebuilding of nearly all of the parish churches in that part of Wiltshire, as well as for the erection of four new churches, including the large

R: WESTMACOTT Fecit 1791.

ornate St Katherine's church which was built for the Savernake estate workers in 1861 to a design by T.H. Wyatt. The church was dedicated to St Katherine by the Marchioness in memory of her mother, Katherine Woronzoff, Countess of Pembroke, who had left money for the building. The nearby church school was also built by the family, and the consecration of the church was celebrated by 'the work people and poor of the district' with a meal of 'beef and pudding' served in the Orangery at Tottenham House.

On the estates in Yorkshire there are many examples of parish churches restored or totally rebuilt at huge expense by the landowners. William Butterfield was commissioned by Viscount Downe to design the large church of St James (1856–8) at Baldersbury Park, and also to produce the plans for the model village with brick-built estate cottages, the village school and fine new vicarage. Lord Hotham spent over £25,000 on a new parish church for his tenants at South Dalton, designed by J.L. Pearson and erected c.1860. Pearson was also employed by Earl Fitzwilliam to design a large new church for his tenants at Wentworth Woodhouse, replacing the medieval parish church of which only the Wentworth chapel survives, crowded with family monuments.[3] The seventh Duke of Newcastle, strongly influenced by the Anglo-Catholic movement within the Church of England, spent £30,000 on the sumptuous church at Clumber Park, erected in 1886–9 to designs by G.F. Bodley. The highly-decorated church, with its profusion of sculptures and stained glass, survives

beside the lake as a splendid feature of the park, although the mansion was demolished in 1938.

An example of the power which a landowner could have over the church on his estate is provided by Ayot St Lawrence (Hertfordshire), where in 1778 the wealthy banker, Sir Lionel Lyde, turned the medieval church into a picturesque ruin and in its place built a new church of unusual design and sited so as to complete the vista at the end of the avenue leading from the house. To reach the new church the parishioner had to make a detour 'so as not to spoil the view from the House'.[4] At Sherbourne (Warwickshire) the large estate

**70** *Great Badminton (Gloucestershire). Monument to the first Duke of Beaufort, 1699. This magnificent and highly-expensive monument, designed by Grinling Gibbons, was originally erected in St George's Chapel, Windsor, but was moved to Badminton in 1875 where a new chancel was added to the church in order to accommodate it.*

**69** *(Left) Sherborne (Gloucestershire). One of the monuments to members of the Dutton family dominating the chancel of the parish church, which is attached to their large mansion. This angel is close to the north side of the altar.*

church was built at a cost of £20,000 by Louisa Ann Rylands, member of a rich Birmingham family who had purchased the estate after making a fortune from wire-drawing. The family also provided brick-built houses with elaborate chimneys and barge-boards and built a school for the village.

In many places architecture and furnishings not in accord with the restorer's conception of 'correctness' were ruthlessly removed, and the interior appearance and atmosphere of churches were completely altered. It was frequently the gentry families who paid for an organ to be installed, replacing the colourful but independent village bands which had previously provided musical accompaniment to services from a west gallery.

Many churches had been allowed to fall into a deplorable state, and urgently needed attention, but the unfortunate result was often the wholesale destruction of ancient pews, screens and galleries, the ruthless scraping of stonework, the innovation of new and highly-coloured glass and tiles and new pine furniture purchased at great expense from approved ecclesiastical suppliers. But while we may regret these drastic restorations, we cannot but admire the energy, enthusiasm and public spirit of those who directed the work and the generosity of those who paid for it.[5] The seating arrangements within the church mirrored exactly the social status of the parishioners with the prominent pew for the gentry, where the family sat on comfortable chairs as though in an elegant drawing room, divorced from their tenants and servants and surrounded by the memorials of their ancestors. In the front sat the farmers and their families in high-sided pews, while the labourers occupied the plain benches at the rear. The liturgy also emphasized the social gradations, while the Catechism proclaimed the Christian duty

To order myself lowly and reverently to all my betters . . . and to do my duty in that state of life, unto which it shall please God to call me.

In many estate villages the parsonage was rebuilt during the eighteenth or nineteenth century, since increasing agricultural production meant a greater tithe income for the clergy, and enclosure also proved to be highly profitable for them. Moreover, many parish livings provided a secure and suitable occupation for a younger son of the estate owner, and a house commensurate with his social status was regarded as essential. Among the large number of people required to work in the house, stables, gardens and park, benevolent landowners often provided light employment for elderly servants or tenants, and many also established almshouses or provided cheap accommodation.

The bequest boards which are often displayed in parish churches bear witness to the charity provided in the form of doles, clothing, blankets or food, and landowners were expected to contribute generously to good causes and to head the subscription lists for local appeals.

## Follies and monuments

Charity of a different sort was provided by some landlords during periods of exceptional difficulty or high unemployment, by hiring men to build 'follies' such as obelisks, pavilions, summer houses or arbours in their grounds. Yorke's Folly near Pateley Bridge (Yorkshire) was built during the eighteenth century to provide employment, as was Sharpe's Folly at Whitton (Northumberland), which is a round tower, 9m (30ft) high, built for Archdeacon Thomas Sharpe and used by him as an observatory. At Barwick near Yeovil (Somerset) the Messiter family provided work for unemployed men during the 1830s in building a number of very tall

**71** *Burton Pynsent (Somerset). The monument overlooking the Somerset Levels, was designed by 'Capability' Brown and erected by William Pitt in 1765 in memory of Sir William Pynsent who had left his estates in Somerset and Wiltshire to Pitt in recognition of his opposition to imposing a tax on cider.*

in the form of a prominent memorial. The great column surmounted by the Percy lion, which was erected at Alnwick in 1816, was the gift of the grateful tenants to the second Duke of Northumberland, who had reduced their rents during a difficult period. The 37m (120ft) high tower on the Yorkshire Wolds near Sledmere was erected in 1865 to Sir Tatton Sykes by 'those who loved him as a friend and honoured him as a landlord'. In the market square at Helmsley (Yorkshire) a tall Gothic monument and statue of Lord Feversham (1798–1867) was erected 'By his

**72** *Hawkesbury (Gloucestershire). Monument (1846) on the Cotswold escarpment to General Lord Robert Somerset, a member of the Beaufort family. This is one of many such monuments erected in prominent situations on estates throughout the south-west of England.*

thin pillars in their park and a Gothic *umbrello* or summer house, surmounted by the figure of Mercury. As with many other such follies, a legend has built up around this figure; it is known locally as Jack the Treacle-Eater and is confidently believed to commemorate a former footman and celebrated runner, who was employed by the family to carry messages, and who owed his amazing speed and stamina to a diet of treacle.[6]

Occasionally the philanthropy of landowners has been repaid by their tenants

Tenantry, Friends and Relatives, who cherish his Memory with Affection and Gratitude'. Among the numerous towers and obelisks on the hill-tops of the south-west is a memorial to generosity of a different sort; this is a tall column designed by Capability Brown, situated at Burton Pynsent in a prominent position overlooking west Sedgemoor (Fig. 71). It was erected by William Pitt, Earl of Chatham, in 1765 to the memory of Sir William Pynsent, who had left his estates in Somerset and Wiltshire to Pitt as a tribute to his success as Prime Minister and because of his earlier opposition to a tax on cider.

## Railways, industries and urban interests

There was not such a great gulf between landowners and industrialists as nineteenth-century novelists sometimes seem to suggest. Many landowners were active in exploiting the industrial potential of their lands, while it was wealth derived from industry, commerce and urban rents which sustained the development of some of the greatest nineteenth-century estates. The Marquess of Westminister's vast estate, immense house and massive establishment at Eaton Hall (Cheshire), one of the greatest examples in Victorian England of the impact of aristocratic ownership upon an entire region, was supported by the proceeds of Welsh mineral royalties and by London ground rents. Similarly, it was industrial wealth which created and supported the estates at Somerleyton (Suffolk), Trentham Hall (Staffordshire), Great Tew (Oxfordshire) and a host of others. At Corsham Court (Wiltshire) much of the Methuen's wealth during the eighteenth and nineteenth centuries came from industrial enterprises and in particular from their ownership of land in the suburbs of Bristol, across which the city expanded in a steady progression of new streets, houses, shops and public houses.

The names of the Georgian and Regency streets and squares around many parts of central London – Berkeley, Portman, Russell, Bedford, Portland, Grosvenor, Bryanston, Eaton and Woburn – are a reminder of the families who profited so greatly from this urban expansion. Likewise, the Calthorpes benefited greatly from the expansion of Birmingham, as did Lord Radnor from the growth of Folkestone, the Tregonwells from the creation of Bournemouth, the Howards at Rotherham, the Duke of Newcastle in Nottingham and the Duke of Norfolk in Sheffield. Many landowners had come to echo the sentiments expressed in the rhyme

> The richest crop for any field
> Is a crop of bricks for it to yield
> The richest crop that it can grow
> Is a crop of houses in a row.[7]

Landowners naturally played a leading part in the massive expansion of the coal industry and in the development of ports. Among them were the Earl of Yarborough at Grimsby, the Duke of Northumberland on Tyneside, the Marquess of Bute at Cardiff, the Duke of Buccleuch at Barrow-in-Furness or Earl Bathurst in Bristol.

Landowners were also quick to recognize the potential profits to be made from railways, especially if they also possessed mineral rights which could be exploited if convenient transport was available. Thus the Basset family in Cornwall, Earl Fitzwilliam in south Yorkshire, the Duke of Buccleuch in Furness and the Duke of Devonshire in Derbyshire were all active in pressing forward the construction of railways. Like many other landowners, they had at first been very reluctant, fearing the intrusion upon their privacy, damage to their parks, interference with agriculture, restriction on hunting and competition with canals in which they had interests. Gradually it became clear that the benefit and profit would outweigh the disadvantages; but many continued to object to the noise, smoke and effect upon their parklands. Their objections were overcome by the generous compensation paid by the railway companies, and by changes to the routes and other concessions which are still very obvious in the modern landscape.

A few stood firm in their opposition, and the seventh Earl of Harborough mounted an armed guard to prevent surveyors planning a route across his estate at Stapleford Park (Leicestershire); eventually the Midland Railway line went around the northern edge of the park by a detour which became known as 'Lord Harborough's Curve'. The Duke of Northumberland similarly refused to allow a railway line to be built through his park at Alnwick. At Shugborough, however, the Earl of Lichfield obtained compensation of £30,000 from the North Staffordshire Railway Company for their line passing through his park, and was able to insist on a deep cutting, tunnels with appropriately elegant entrances and bridges with high sides so that his horses should not be frightened; he was provided with his own station, designed to his own requirements by the architect John Livock, nearby at Colwich. Four identical stations were built on the Duke of Bedford's estate at Woburn designed as romantic-looking cottages with gables, barge-boards and half-timbering. The Midland Railway in the Peak District passed through numerous estates and parks, and stations had to be provided at Bakewell for the Duke of Rutland of Haddon Hall; and in return for allowing the railway to come through the Chatsworth estate, the Duke of Devonshire had stations designed to his own satisfaction at Rowsley, Matlock and Hassop. At Brocklesby (Lincolnshire) the station architecture was made to match the distinctive style of Lord Yarborough's estate.

Lord Fitzwilliam lodged many objections to the proposed route of the Great Northern railway from King's Cross to York, and among them was his insistence on a detour being made around his woodland coverts near Peterborough in order that the foxes should not be disturbed and his hunting ruined.[8] The main railway line from South Wales to London is concealed in a shallow tunnel as it passes through the Duke of Beaufort's estate at Badminton, and the ventilation shafts marking the route of the tunnel are disguised as castellated towers. By the 1850s a line was even laid across the grasslands of Leicestershire, traversing the finest hunting country in England.

> Above the fields of Leicestershire
> On arches we were borne
> And the rumble of the railway drowned
> The thunder of the Quorn.[9]

## Visitors

For several centuries many of the great houses and spreading parklands have been open to visitors and travellers; and those who were perceived by the lodge-keepers, housekeepers and other servants to be of gentry status generally had little difficulty in gaining access. John Leland in the sixteenth century and Celia Fiennes in the late seventeenth century visited many houses and parks in their journeys through England. By the eighteenth century the practice of visiting the great houses and their gardens was growing rapidly in popularity, and servants began to expect payment for showing visitors over the house, while gardens such as those at Stourhead and Stowe were designed from the first with the idea of being visited. Even for a fairly modest garden like that of Thomas Goldney at Clifton on the heights above Bristol, tickets were issued which entitled visitors to be conducted around the grounds and the grotto by the gardener, Adam Sixsmith.

Improved facilities for travel during the nineteenth century brought more and more visitors to the famous houses, and formal arrangements began to be made to cater for the increased numbers. Houses and grounds such as Castle Howard, Chatsworth, Holkham Hall, Hampton Court, Blenheim and many others were open at set times and on an organized basis. From the mid-eighteenth century enterprising local printers produced guide books to assist the visitor. For example, a description of the house and gardens at Stowe was produced in 1744 and new editions were frequently issued thereafter. Journals and descriptions of tours made through various parts of England became an increasingly popular literary form. Owners were proud that their fine houses and carefully tended grounds should be visited by persons of taste and discernment. The gardens at Stourhead were opened by Henry Hoare as soon as the landscaping, planting and building commenced during the 1740s, and nearby inn, The Spread Eagle provided accommodation for tourists.

As early as 1751 a guidebook to Wilton House (Wiltshire) was produced, and was sold in London, Bath and Salisbury, providing '*A Description of the Pictures, Statues, Busto's, Bass-Relievo's, and Other Curiosities at the Earl of Pembroke's House at Wilton*'. The task of showing visitors over a great house became a valuable perquisite of the housekeeper and other household servants. A visitor to Wilton in 1776 noted that according to the porter's book 2324 persons had visited the house during the previous year, and by the early nineteenth century the tips which ranged from 2s 6d to £1 0s 0d from each party of visitors were collected and shared out in varying amounts between the housekeeper, butler, housemaids and other indoor servants. Not all servants were equally proficient as tour guides, and in 1827 Lord Pembroke wrote to the housekeeper '. . . complaints have been

made of how ill the house is shown, the Maid who used to show it not having had sense enough to pull the blinds up during the time that People were looking at the Pictures'.[10]

Increasing numbers of visitors also made life intolerable for owners and their families and brought problems of theft, vandalism and damage which have become all too familiar in the twentieth century. In 1783 Horace Walpole complained bitterly of the disturbance caused by visitors to his celebrated house and gardens at Strawberry Hill near Twickenham, and was frequently amazed at their uncouth behaviour, 'I am tormented all day and every day by people that come to see my house, and have no enjoyment of it in summer'.[11] One possible solution was to make a charge for entry and to price this beyond the means of undesirable visitors. Apparently this was already being tried at Lulworth Castle (Dorset) in 1853 as the following printed notice illustrates:

### NOTICE

Persons About To Visit
LULWORTH
CASTLE

Are hereby informed that in consequence of the mischief done by certain persons who have been brought thither by the Steamers from Weymouth, during the past Summer, and their otherwise misconduct, the Owner of the Castle is under the necessity of ordering an admittance fee of ONE SHILLING each, to be paid to the person who shews it; and if this does not remedy the evil complained of and ensure a more orderly class of Visitors, the Castle will not in future be shewn but by an Order from the Owner

*Dated, Lulworth, September 26th, 1853.*[12]

A few benevolent landlords positively encouraged local people to enjoy their parks, and the grounds of Arundel (Sussex), Cirencester (Gloucestershire), Eaton Hall

(Cheshire) and many others were freely open to the public. At Blenheim the inhabitants of Woodstock had their own gateway to the park. Even more welcoming was the celebrated archaeologist General Pitt Rivers, who during the late nineteenth century provided on his estate at Tollard Royal on the borders of Wiltshire and Dorset, a large recreation park known as the Larmer Grounds. There the General provided shelters for picnics with crockery and cutlery supplied, but alcoholic drinks prohibited, gardens, a lake, formal walks, a theatre and a bandstand. Workmen from the estate formed the band which performed on Sunday afternoons during the summer. The Larmer Grounds became very popular and in 1893 24,000 people visited the grounds.[13]

## The decline of the great estates

In spite of the agricultural depression of the later nineteenth century, taxation, death duties, the sharp decline in estate incomes and the financial difficulties faced by many landowners, the creation of new country houses and landscaped parks continued up to the eve of the First World War in 1914.

**73** *The Vyne (Hampshire). Foxhounds setting off from a meet during the 1930s, the number and variety of the participants showing the way in which hunting remained a focus of interest for all classes in the rural community. (Rural History Centre, University of Reading.)*

**74**   *Bratton (Wiltshire). Departure for the First World War, August 1914. This faded photograph captures the end of the old rural England. It shows the young men of Bratton and district being taken away in the cars of the local gentry to enlist at Devizes. Many of these volunteers were never to return, and those who did came back to a very different environment, with the great landowners and their estates in rapid decline.*

Examples include Sandringham (Norfolk) created by Edward, Prince of Wales during the 1860s with an estate village at West Newton. A major purpose of Sandringham was to allow the Prince to indulge his passion for game shooting, and the woodlands were planned and under-planted with the rearing of game in mind, and vast sums were spent on pheasants and the protection of partridges and hares. The result was the massive increase in the number shot each year and totals rose from some 7000 in 1870 to more than 30,000 in 1910. The Duke of Westminster's estate at Eaton Hall continued to provide a model of lavish expenditure and total control of all aspects of the life of tenants and servants. Fifty servants were employed in the mansion, and 40 gardeners, the estate also possessed its own gas-works and a narrow-gauge railway. Between 1869 and 1899 four churches, eight parsonages and 15 schools were built on the estate as well as 50 farms and more than 300 cottages, a building programme which profoundly affects the appearance and character of that part of Cheshire.[14]

In Berkshire, Bear Wood, an enormous mansion between Reading and Wokingham was built for John Walter, owner of *The Times*, to the design of Robert Kerr in 1865–8 at a cost of over £120,000. An estate village was also built to house the large number of indoor and outdoor servants necessary to run such a huge establishment. This was the new village of Sindlesham Green built at the gates of the park and around a triangular green; the position and the picturesque, uniform architecture are testimony to estate ownership, and even the village inn is named the Walter Arms. The whole complex of Bear Wood and the surrounding villages provides an excellent example of a large and wealthy late-Victorian estate.

Other examples include Buscot (Berkshire), where the house was greatly enlarged and a model village constructed for Lord Faringdon during the 1890s, and Bryanston (Dorset) where the large house was built for Lord Portman in *c.*1890, using wealth derived from the family's London rents. Bryanston was designed by Norman Shaw, and its stark, uncompromising outline, emphasized by the bright red of its brick-work, dominates the town of Blandford Forum and all the surrounding countryside.

During the twentieth century there were far fewer landowners who could afford to run such great houses, and scarcely any who would have contemplated building on such a scale. One exception is Castle Drogo (Devon), a great house constructed entirely of granite and designed by Sir Edward Lutyens for Julius Drewe, who had made a vast fortune as the founder of the chain of grocery shops known as the Home and Colonial Stores. It was built during the period 1910 to 1930 on a dramatic site on the edge of Dartmoor. Another is Middleton Park (Oxfordshire), also designed on a grand scale by Lutyens and built in 1938 for the Earl of Jersey, including landscaped

grounds, lodges and rebuilt village cottages in the traditional manner. By this time it was much more common for landowners to seek for ways of disposing of their houses and estates, and the National Trust, which was to prove the salvation of so many houses, parks and estate landscapes, was founded in 1895. At first the intention was to preserve open spaces and landscapes, but later the Trust also acquired historic buildings and rapidly became the major force in the preservation of a remarkable heritage which would otherwise have inevitably been lost by demolition of the buildings and destruction of the carefully created landscapes.

The effects of agricultural depression, taxes, death duties, and the loss of so many male heirs during the First World War of 1914–18 (Fig. 74), together with all the subsequent economic and social changes, brought about the break up of many of the grandest estates and the abandonment of their mansions. In their place have come country parks, owner-occupied farms and institutional uses for the houses. A recent study of a sample of country houses in the East Midlands has shown the changes that took place between 1880 and 1980 (see table below).[15]

It is appropriate to end this survey of the long history of estates in the landscape by an example of the fate which, without the National Trust, would have befallen a great

A sample of country houses in the East Midlands

| County | Number of houses | Demolished | Still in private ownership | Institutional ownership |
|---|---|---|---|---|
| Derbyshire | 10 | 2 | 5 | 2 |
| Leicestershire | 8 | 4 | 3 | 1 |
| Lincolnshire | 16 | 7 | 6 | 3 |
| Nottinghamshire | 9 | 2 | 3 | 4 |
| Rutland | 3 | 0 | 3 | 0 |

number of the major houses of England, and of the way in which, despite the destruction of the house, the effect of centuries of ownership by a single family is still very apparent in the landscape. The house was Houndstreet, in the parish of Marksbury, 8km (5 miles) south-west of Bath.

Throughout the Middle Ages the estate had been part of the vast possession of Glastonbury Abbey; some years after the Dissolution it was purchased by Sir John Popham, Lord Chief Justice, and remained in the possession of the Popham family until 1925. Their influence on the landscape can be seen in the surrounding villages which were part of the estate, with farms and cottages unmistakably built in the same 'estate' style, many bearing a large letter 'P' as further evidence of their origin and ownership. Next to the park around the site of the Popham's house is the estate village, built in a consciously picturesque style to accommodate the household servants, estate steward and other officials and including Park Farm, which provided milk and provisions for the house. All around are the landscaped grounds, carefully-planned woodlands, a chain of six lakes and the site of a gazebo or summer house giving an extensive view over part of the estate. But the Popham house no longer exists.

During the 1770s Francis Popham, who then owned the estate, decided to build a huge new mansion to replace the early seventeenth-century house which he had inherited. The new house was built of Bath stone and was 17 bays wide. No expense was spared in either building or furnishing; elaborate plaster-work, statues, carvings and decoration were included, while gardens, a long, sweeping carriage drive and avenues of trees were laid out to lend dignity to the approach. A large stable building, carriage-houses and an ice-house were constructed, and a large kitchen garden was created. Francis Popham died in 1779 long before the vast project was completed, but the work

was energetically continued by his widow, Dorothy, until her death in 1797, by which time most of the house was complete. They had no children and all the property, including the great mansion passed to a relative, General Leyborne Popham, who lived at the family's other mansion, Littlecote in Wiltshire. Houndstreet House, therefore, remained empty and unused and deteriorated very rapidly. In 1822 the Revd John Skinner, the antiquarian and archaeologist, who was rector of the nearby parish of Camerton, visited Houndstreet to picnic by the lakes, and wrote that

Although upwards of thirty thousand pounds were expended on the Mansion and Grounds not many years since, the whole is fast going to decay . . . the noble piece of water is covered with weeds and long grass; thistles and nettles cover the walks . . .[16]

By 1831 the house was in such a bad state that General Leyborne Popham ordered a survey to be made. This reported that the roof had been leaking, much of the woodwork had rotted, part of the plaster ceilings had fallen and that very large sums would have to be spent before the house could be made habitable. The General decided that the only sensible course was to demolish the house, in spite of the huge sums that had been spent to build it. The stable block was kept and turned into a much smaller house, but the great mansion was totally demolished, except for six pillars which had formed the drawing room windows. These were kept as a curious feature in the grounds of the smaller house, and now stand incongruously in the middle of a grass field as a witness to the great and vastly expensive mansion which stood there, a reminder of the wealth which landowners were prepared to lavish on such symbols of power and status, and as a dramatic illustration of how quickly and completely such a massive structure can disappear from the English landscape.[17]

# Notes

**Introduction** (pages 11–13)

1. D. Bonney, 'Early Boundaries and Estates in Southern England', in P.H. Sawyer (ed.), *English Medieval Settlement*, Edward Arnold, 1979; M. Aston, *Interpreting the Landscape*, Batsford, 1985, 32–43.
2. *Return of Owners of Land* 1872–3, Parliamentary Papers, LXXII. The statistics were analysed and rearranged in J. Bateman, *Great Landowners of Great Britain*, 1876, Leicester University Press, new ed. 1971.
3. F.M.L. Thompson, *English Landed Society in the Nineteenth Century*, Routledge & Kegan Paul, 1963; H.A. Clemenson, *English Country Houses and Landed Estates*, Croom Helm, 1982.

**Chapter 1** (pages 15–28)

1. T. Rowley, *The Norman Heritage 1066–1200*, Routledge & Kegan Paul, 1983, 36–57; R. Morris, *Churches in the Landscape*, Dent, 1989; R.A. Brown, *English Castles*, Batsford, 1976; N.J.G. Pounds, *The Medieval Castle in England and Wales*, Cambridge U.P., 1990.
2. H.C. Darby (ed.), *Domesday England*, Cambridge U.P., 1977; J.H. Bettey, *Wessex from AD 1000*, Longman, 1986, 26.
3. R. Lennard, *Rural England 1086–1135*, Oxford University Press, 1959; P.A. Stamper, 'The Medieval Forest of Pamber', *Landscape History* 5, 1983, 41–52; M. Aston, *Interpreting the Landscape*, Batsford, 1985, 111–12.
4. C. Taylor, 'Whiteparish, the development of a forest-edge parish', *Wiltshire Archaeological Magazine*, 62, 1967, 79–102.
5. J.H. Bettey, *Wessex from AD 1000*, Longman, 1986, 15, 47.
6. L. Cantor, 'Forests, Chases, Parks and Warrens', in L. Cantor (ed.), *The English Medieval Landscape*, Croom Helm, 1982, 56–85.
7. D. Hey, *Yorkshire from AD 1000*, Longman, 1986, 81–2.
8. M.B. Rowlands, *The West Midlands from AD 1000*, Longman, 1987, 33.
9. Register of Wolston de Bransford, bishop of Worcester 1339–49, *Worcestershire Historical Society*, NS, 4, 1966, 194–5; K.C. Newton, *The Manor of Writtle*, Phillimore, 1970, 28–30, 44–5.
10. L. Cantor, 'Forests, Chases, Parks and Warrens', in L. Cantor (ed.), *The English Medieval Landscape*, Croom Helm, 1982, 56–85.
11. C.J. Bond, 'Monastic Fisheries' in M. Aston (ed.), *Medieval Fish, Fisheries and Fishponds in England*, BAR Bristol Series 182(i), 1988, 69–112; H.P.R. Finberg, *Tavistock Abbey*, David & Charles, 1969, 166.
12. C.J. Bond, 'Monastic Fisheries' in M. Aston (ed.), *Medieval Fish, Fisheries and Fishponds in England*, BAR Bristol Series 182(i), 1988, 77; K.L. Wood-Legh, *A Small Household of the Fifteenth Century*, Manchester U.P., 1953.
13. M. Aston (ed.), *Medieval Fish, Fisheries and Fishponds in England*, BAR Bristol Series 182(i), 1988, i, 40, ii, 309; P. Bigmore, *The Bedfordshire and Huntingdonshire Landscape*,

Hodder & Stoughton, 1979, 96–7.

14. C.F. Hickling, 'Prior More's Fishponds', *Medieval Archaeology*, 15, 1971, 118–22; E.S. Fegan (ed.), 'Journal of Prior William More', *Worcestershire Historical Society*, 1914.

15. *R.C.H.M. Northamptonshire*, II, 1979, 75–7.

16. *R.C.H.M. Northamptonshire*, IV, 1982, 132–4.

17. 'Register of Adam de Orleton, bishop of Worcester 1327–33' *Worcestershire Historical Society*, NS, 10, 1979, 142.

18. J.H. Bettey, *Suppression of the Monasteries in the West Country*, Alan Sutton, 1989, 98, 185.

19. M. Aston, *Interpreting the Landscape*, Batsford, 1985, 114–16; J. Bond, 'Rabbits', *The Local Historian*, 18, 1988, 53–7; H.E. Hallam, (ed.), *Agrarian History of England and Wales*, II, 1042–1350, Cambridge University Press, 1988, 943, 945–6; A. Harris and D. Spratt, 'Some Yorkshire Rabbit Warrens', *Current Archaeology*, 125, 1991, 204–7; J. Sheail, *Rabbits & Their History*, David & Charles, 1972; T. Williams and R. Loveday, 'Rabbits or Ritual' *The Archaeological Journal*, 145, 1988, 290–313.

20. S.F. Hockey, *Quarr Abbey and its Lands 1132–1631*, Leicester U.P., 1970, 194–7.

21. H.P.R. Finberg, *Tavistock Abbey*, David & Charles, 1969, 92; C.J. Bond, 'The Estates of Abingdon Abbey', *Landscape History*, I, 1979, 59–75.

22. J. Thirsk (ed.), *Agrarian History of England*, Cambridge University Press, IV, 1967, 676; Dorset Record Office, D10/M71, Hatfield House, Salisbury MSS, Accounts 133/8; M.E. Field, 'Five Northamptonshire Families', *Northamptonshire Record Society*, XIX, 1956, 75–6.

23. Public Record Office, CP40/2611; STAC 2/27/46.

24. J.H. Bettey (ed.), 'Correspondence of the Smyth Family of Ashton Court 1548–1642', *Bristol Record Society*, XXXV, 1982, 37.

25. *Historical Manuscripts Commission*, 'Dean and Chapter of Wells MSS' I, 1907, 425–8; J.M. Steane, *The Northamptonshire Landscape*, Hodder & Stoughton, 1974, 179.

26. H.E. Hallam (ed.), *Agrarian History of England and Wales*, II, Cambridge University Press, 882–5, 945.

27. R. Holt, *Mills in Medieval England*, 1988; J. Bond, *Medieval Windmills in South-Western England*, forthcoming

**Chapter 2** (pages 29–44)

1. P. Brandon and B. Short, *The South-East from AD 1000*, Longman, 1990, 114.

2. O. Rackham, *The History of the Countryside*, Dent, 1986, 360–4; F.A. Aberg (ed.), *Medieval Moated Sites*, C.B.A. Research Report No. 17, 1978.

3. J. Harvey, *Medieval Gardens*, Batsford, 1981; T. McLean, *Medieval English Gardens*, Collins, 1981; S.F. Hockey (ed.), 'The Beaulieu Cartulary', *Southampton Record Series*, 17, 1974; T.J. Hunt and I. Kiel, 'Two Medieval Gardens' *Somerset Natural History and Archaeological Society Proceedings*, 104, 1959–60, 91–101. This whole subject will be discussed in detail in T. Williamson and A. Taigel, *Parks and Gardens*, Batsford, forthcoming.

4. T. McLean. *Medieval English Gardens*. Collins, 1981, 99–101.

5. J. Fowler, *Medieval Sherborne*, Longmans, Dorchester, 1951, 106.

6. C.J. Bond, 'The Estates of Abingdon Abbey', *Landscape History*, I, 1979, 59–75.

7. P. Brandon and B. Short, *The South-East from AD 1000*, Longman, 1990, 69.

8. J.H. Bettey, *Suppression of the Monasteries in the West Country*, Alan Sutton, 1989, 98.

9. C. Platt, *Medieval England*, Routledge & Kegan Paul, 1978, 172.

10. D. Hey, *Yorkshire from AD 1000*, Longman, 1986, 65.

11. J.H. Bettey, *Wessex from AD 1000*, Longman, 1986, 43–4.

12. B. Jennings (ed.), *History of Nidderdale*, Advertiser Press, Huddersfield, 1967, 38–9.

13. C. Platt, *The Monastic Grange in Medieval England*, Macmillan, 1969, 183–245.

14. W. Horn and E. Born, *Great Coxwell Barn*, University of California, 1965.

15. M. Aston, *Interpreting the Landscape*, Batsford, 1985, 86–90.

16. B. Bailey, *Almshouses*, Robert Hale, 1988, 45–74.

17. M.W. Beresford, *New Towns of the Middle Ages*, Lutterworth Press, 1967; M.W. Beresford, 'Six New Towns of the Bishops of Winchester *Medieval Archaeology*, 3, 1959, 187–215.

**Chapter 3** (pages 45–57)

1. J.H. Bettey, *Suppression of the Monasteries in the West Country*, Alan Sutton, 1989, 100.

2. J. Harvey, *Medieval Gardens*, Batsford, 1981, 136–40.

3. R. Strong, *The Renaissance Garden in England*, Thames & Hudson, 1979, 24.

4. J. Harvey, *Medieval Gardens*, Batsford, 1981, 135–6.

5. R. Strong, *The Renaissance Garden in England*, Thames & Hudson, 51–7.

6. *Royal Commission on Historic Monuments, Northamptonshire*, III, 1981, 103–9.

7. W.D. Christie, *Life of the First Earl of Shaftesbury*, 1871, I, xv; *Royal Commission on Historical Manuscripts*, Various Collections, iii, xxxv–lvii; L. Stone and J.C.F. Stone, *An Open Elite? England 1540–1880*, Oxford University Press, 1984, 314–15.

8. M.W. Beresford, *The Lost Villages of England*, Alan Sutton, 1983; M. Aston, *Interpreting the Landscape*, Batsford, 1985, 53–70; C. Dyer, 'Deserted Medieval Villages in the West Midlands', *Economic History Review*, 2nd. Ser., XXXV, 1982, 19–34.

9. L.M. Munby, *The Hertfordshire Landscape*, Hodder & Stoughton, 1977, 133–4; D.M. Palliser, *The Staffordshire Landscape*, Hodder & Stoughton, 1976, 96.

10. Public Record Office, C2/James I C2/62; *Royal Commission on Historic Monuments, Dorset*, IV, 20; R.H. Tawney, *The Agrarian Problem in the Sixteenth Century*, 1967, 201.

11. P. Bigmore, *The Bedfordshire and Huntingdonshire Landscape*, Hodder & Stoughton, 1979, 125.

12. M.B. Rowlands, *The West Midlands from AD 1000*, Longman, 1987, 71; C.J. Bond, 'Deserted Medieval Villages in Warwickshire and Worcestershire', in T.R. Slater and P.J. Jarvis (eds), *Field and Forest*, Norwich, 1982.

13. P. Brandon and B. Short, *The South-East from AD 1000*, Longman, 1990, 179.

14. J.H. Bettey, 'Economic Pressures and Village Desertions in South Dorset' *Somerset & Dorset Notes & Queries*, XXXIII, 1991, 3–6.

15. J.H. Bettey, 'The Cultivation of Woad in the Salisbury Area during the Sixteenth and Seventeenth Centuries', *Textile History*, 9, 1978, 112–17.

16. Richard Carew, *Survey of Cornwall*, 1602.

17. Thomas Fuller, *Worthies of England*, 1952 ed.

18. D.G.C. Allen, 'The Rising in the West 1628–31'. *Economic History Review*, 2nd. Ser., 5, 1952, 76–85; J.H. Bettey, 'The Revolts over the Enclosure of the Royal Forest of Gillingham', *Dorset Natural History and Archaeological Society Proceedings*, 97, 1975–6, 21–4.

19. L.M. Munby, *The Landscape of Hertfordshire*, Hodder & Stoughton, 1977, 139.

20. K.S.H. Wyndham, 'In Pursuit of Crown Land' *Somerset Archaeological Society Proceedings*, 123, 1979, 65–74; P. Brandon and B. Short, *The South-East from AD 1000*, 1990, 135–6; L.M. Munby, *The Hertfordshire Landscape* Hodder & Stoughton, 1976, 154.

21. D. Hey, *Yorkshire from AD 1000*, Longman, 1986, 127.

22. J.H. Bettey, *The Suppression of the Monasteries in the West Country* Alan Sutton, 1989, 123–4.

23. J.R. Wordie, 'Social Change on the Leveson-Gower Estates 1714–183, *Economic History Review*, 2nd. Ser., XXVII, 1974, 593–609; D.M. Palliser, *The Staffordshire Landscape*, Hodder & Stoughton, 1976, 95–6.

24. J.H. Bettey, *Wessex from AD 1000*, Longman, 1986, 181–5.

**Chapter 4** (pages 58–82)

1. R. Strong, *The Renaissance Garden in England*, Thames & Hudson, 1979, 45–112.
2. M.E. Finch, *Five Northamptonshire Families*, Northants. Record Society, XX, 1956, 156.
3. P.R.O., C2/Jas I C2/62; C2/Jas I C26/36; J. Hutchins, *History of Dorset*, 1861–70, III, 670–9; C. Cross (ed.), 'The Letters of Sir Francis Hastings 1574–1609', *Somerset Record Society*, LXIX, 1969, 28–30; M. Aston, 'Gardens and Earthworks at Hardington and Low Ham', *Somerset Archaeological and Natural History Proceedings*, 122, 1978, 11–17.
4. C. Morris (ed.), *The Journeys of Celia Fiennes*, Cresset Press, 1947, 90, 97, 335–6.
5. L. Munby, *The Hertfordshire Landscape*, Hodder & Stoughton, 1977, 150–1; R. Strong, *The Renaissance Garden in England*, Thames & Hudson, 1979, 104–7. For details of the extent and cost of Robert Cecil's building work, as well as of the expenses of laying out his gardens see L. Stone, *Family and Fortune*, Oxford University Press, 1973, 62–91. Stone calculated that between 1607 and 1612 Cecil spent about £60,000 on buildings and gardens.
6. J. Aubrey, *Brief Lives*, Secker & Warburg, 1950 ed., 13–15.
7. F. Bamford (ed.), *A Royalist's Notebook, the Commonplace Book of Sir John Oglander of Nunwell, 1622–52*, 1936, 84–95; P.R.O. 30/24/5 Earl of Shaftesbury's Book of Memorandums.
8. R. Strong, *The Renaissance Garden in England*, Thames & Hudson, 1979, 122.
9. C. Taylor, *The Cambridgeshire Landscape*, Hodder & Stoughton, 1973, 163–4.
10. W. Rollinson, *A History of Cumberland and Westmorland*, Phillimore, 1978, 64–5.
11. *Ibid.*, 142–4.
12. B. Bailey, *Almshouses*, Robert Hale, 1988, 103–140.
13. J. Thirsk (ed.), *Agrarian History of England & Wales, IV, 1500–1640*, Cambridge U.P., 1967, 161–196; J. Thirsk (ed.), *Agrarian History of England & Wales, V(ii), 1640–1750*, Cambridge University Press, 1985, 533–86.
14. Dorset Record Office, D10/M71; L. Keen (ed.), *Historic Landscape of the Weld Estate*, Dorset County Council, 1987.
15. S. Collier, *Whitehaven 1660–1800*, Royal Commission on Historical Monuments of England, 1991.
16. F. Bamford (ed.), *A Royalist Notebook, the Commonplace Book of Sir John Oglande of Nunwell, 1622–52*, 1936, 75.
17. G.E. Mingay, *The Gentry*, Longman, 1976, 98.
18. C. Morris (ed.), *The Journals of Celia Fiennes*, Cresset Press, 1947, 173–6.

**Chapter 5** (pages 83–108)

1. G.E. Mingay, *The Gentry*, Longman, 1976, 21–2.
2. C. Morris (ed.), *The Journeys of Celia Fiennes*, Cresset Press, 1947, 55, 67–8, 151, 233; D. Defoe, *Tour*, Everyman ed., 1927, I, 167–8. This whole subject will be dealt with in more detail in T. Williamson and A. Taigel, *Parks and Gardens*, Batsford, forthcoming.
3. C. Taylor, *Dorset*, Hodder & Stoughton, 1990, 144–5.
4. C. Hussey, *English Gardens and Landscapes 1700–1750*, Country Life, 1976. H.C. Prince, *Parks in England*, Shalfleet Manor (IOW), 1967.
5. M. Jourdain, *The Work of William Kent*, Country Life, 1948.
6. D. Stroud, *Capability Brown*, Country Life, 1950.
7. Humphry Repton, *Fragment on the Theory and Practice of Landscape Gardening*, 1816 ed., 38–9, 150; D. Stroud, *Humphry Repton*, Country Life, 1962.
8. J. Bond and K. Tiller, *Blenheim, Landscape for a Palace*, Alan Sutton, 1987, 90–113.
9. D. Stroud, *Capability Brown*, Country Life, 1957, 51–2.
10. G.E. Mingay (ed.), *Agrarian History of England & Wales, VI, 1750–1850*, Cambridge

University Press, 1989, 566–71; J.V. Beckett, *The Aristocracy in England 1660–1914*, Blackwell, 1986, 323–37.

11. F.J. Ladd, *Architects at Corsham Court*, Moonraker Press, 1978, 69–74, 112–13.

12. L. Stone and J.C.F. Stone, *An Open Elite? England 1540–1880*, Oxford University Press, 1984, 104; T. Rowley, *The Shropshire Landscape*, Hodder & Stoughton, 1972, 127–9.

13. J.H. Bettey, *Wessex from AD 1000*, Longman, 1986, 211; J. Lees-Milne, *William Beckford*, Tisbury, 1976; K. Woodbridge, *Landscape and Antiquity: Aspects of English Culture at Stourhead*, Oxford University Press, 1970.

14. L. Whistler, *Guide to Stowe Garden*, 1956; H.F. Clark, *The English Landscape Garden*, Pleiades Books, 1948; J.M. Robinson, *Temples of Delight, Stowe Landscape Gardens*, National Trust, 1990.

15. R.J.G. Savage, 'Natural History of the Goldney Garden Grotto, Clifton, Bristol', *Garden History*, 17, 1989, 1–40; J.H. Bettey, *Bristol Observed*, Redcliffe Press, 1986, 74–7.

16. J.M. Robinson, *Temples of Delight, Stowe Landscape Gardens*, National Trust, 1990, 134–40.

17. C.S. Smith, *The Building of Castle Howard*, Faber & Faber, 1990, 121; D. Dymond, *The Norfolk Landscape*, Hodder & Stoughton, 1985, 194.

18. M.A. Clemenson, *English Country Houses and Landed Estates*, Croom Helm, 1982, 76–7.

19. J.H. Bettey, *Wessex from AD 1000*, Longman, 1986, 213; J. Brocklebank, *Affpuddle in Dorset*, Commin (Bournemouth), 1968, 62.

20. P.J. Jarvis, 'Plant Introductions to England' in H.S.A. Fox and R.A. Butlin (eds), *Change in the Countryside*, Institute of British Geographers, 1979, 145–64.

21. R. Carr, *English Foxhunting*, Weidenfeld & Nicolson, 1976; D. Itzkowitz, *Peculiar Privilege*, Harvester Press, 1977.

22. F.M.L. Thompson, *English Landed Society in the Nineteenth Century*, Routledge & Kegan Paul, 1963, 97, 136–50.

23. J.H. Bettey, *Wessex from AD 1000*, Longman, 1986, 197–203.

24. D. Defoe, *Tour through England and Wales*, Everyman Ed., I, 187, 28.

25. A. Young, *A Six Week's Tour*, 1768, 21.

26. O. Wilkinson, *The Agricultural Revolution in the East Riding of Yorkshire*, East Yorkshire Local History Society, 1956, 13–14; C.S. Orwin and R.J. Sellick, *The Reclamation of Exmoor Forest*, Oxford University Press, 1970; M. Havinden, *The Somerset Landscape*, Hodder & Stoughton, 1981, 180–7.

27. J.M. Martin, *Georgian Model Farms*, Oxford University Press, 1983; S. Wade-Martins, *Historic Farm Buildings*, Batsford, 1991.

28. J.T. Ward and R.G. Wilson, *Land and Industry*, David & Charles, 1971, 16–62.

29. L. Munby, *The Hertfordshire Landscape*, Hodder & Stoughton, 1977, 208–9; D.M. Palliser, *The Staffordshire Landscape*, Hodder & Stoughton, 1976, 244–5; C. Hadfield, *The Canals of Southern England*, Phoenix House, 1955.

30. Edward Hughes, 'The Eighteenth-Century Estate Agent', in H.A. Cronne *et al.* (eds), *Essays in British and Irish History*, Muller, 1949, 185–99; Dorset Record Office, D1/MO 3.; J. Wake (ed.), 'The Letters of Daniel Eaton 1725–32', *Northamptonshire Record Society*, XXIV, 1971.

31. J.H. Bettey, *Wessex from AD 1000*, Longman, 1986, 200–4.

32. P. Brandon and B. Short, *The South East from AD 1000*, Longman, 1990, 223–4.

33. Dorset Record Office, D1/MO 3, Survey of the Estate of Thomas Brand Hollis 1799.

## Chapter 6 (pages 109–31)

1. L. Stone and J.C.F. Stone, *An Open Elite? England 1540–1880*, Oxford University Press, 1984, 330.

2. D. Hey, *Yorkshire from AD 1000*, Longman, 1986, 205; D.M. Palliser, *The Staffordshire Landscape*, Hodder & Stoughton, 1976, 133–4.

3. F.J. Ladd, *Architects at Corsham Court*, Moonraker Press, 1978, 112–13.

4. Dorset Record Office, Q.S.M. 1/17, Quarter Sessions Order Book 1754–71, 4 October 1763.

5. *Royal Commission of Historical Monuments (England)*, Dorset II(i), 1970, 171; J.H. Bettey, *Dorset*, David & Charles, 1974, 171; C. Taylor, *The Making of the English Landscape: Dorset*, Hodder & Stoughton, 1970, 176–7; Dorset Record Office, D311/1; D1/NL/a, Plans of Milton Abbas, *c*.1770 and 1799.

6. R. Christian, *Derbyshire*, Batsford, 1978, 115; D.M. Palliser, *The Staffordshire Landscape* Hodder & Stoughton, 1976, 134–6; L. Munby, *The Hertfordshire Landscape*, Hodder & Stoughton, 1977, 157.

7. D. Dymond, *The Norfolk Landscape*, Hodder & Stoughton, 1985, 192–9.

8. K.A. Allison, *The East Riding of Yorkshire Landscape*, Hodder & Stoughton, 1976, 184–7.

9. On the subject of lodges and entrances to estates see T. Mowl: T. Mowl and B. Earnshaw, *Trumpet at a Distant Gate*, Waterstone, 1985.

10. J.H. Bettey, *Bristol Observed*, Redcliffe Press, 1986, 95–6.

11. W. Cobbett, *Rural Rides*, Everyman Ed., 1927, II, 78.

12. Quoted by G.E. Fussell, *The English Rural Labourer*, 1949, 45.

13. W. Cobbett, *Rural Rides*, Everyman Ed., 1927, II, 55.

14. Parliamentary Papers 1867.

15. Royal Commission on the Housing of the Working Class, 1884–5, Vol. 30. I am grateful to my colleague Robert Machin for providing me with information from this Report.

16. *The Rural World*, 15 May 1900; M. Havinden, 'The Model Village' in G.E. Mingay, (ed.), *The Victorian Countryside*, 1981, 414–27.

17. P. Horn, 'An Eighteenth-Century Land Agent: the Career of Nathaniel Kent 1737–1810', *Agricultural History Review*, XXX, 1982.

18. M.L. Sino, *Loudon and the Landscape*, Yale U.P., 1988; Royal Commission on the Housing of the Working Class, 1884–5. Vol. 30.

19. G.E. Mingay (ed.), *The Agrarian History of England and Wales*, VI, Cambridge University Press, 1989, 745.

20. M. Girouard, *The Victorian Country House*, Oxford University Press, 1971, 74.

21. T.W. Beastall, *The Agricultural Revolution in Lincolnshire*, History of Lincolnshire Committee, 1978, 218.

22. M.A. Havinden, *Estate Villages*, University of Reading, 1966, 51–75; J.M. Robinson, *The English Country Estate*, The National Trust, 1988, 86–112; S. Wade Martins, *A Great Estate at Work: The Holkham Estate and Its Inhabitants in the Nineteenth Century*, Cambridge University Press, 1980.

23. For detailed study of the whole subject see G. Darley, *Villages of Vision*, Architectural Press, 1975, especially 61–88.

24. S. Wade Martins, *Historic Farm Buildings*, Batsford, 1991; R. Brigden, *Victorian Farms*, Crowood Press, Ramsbury, 1986.

25. J.M. Robinson, *Georgian Model Farms*, Oxford University Press, 1983.

26. R. Hellier and B. Hutton, 'A Model Farm at Scarthingwell near York', *Agricultural History Review*, 35, 1987, 72–5; S. Macdonald, 'Model Farms' in G.E. Mingay, (ed.), *The Victorian Countryside*, 1981, II, 214–26.

27. J.H. Bettey, *Wessex from AD 1000*, Longman, 1986, 255–7.

28. C. Miller, 'Whitfield Example Farm: A Victorian Model', *Bristol Industrial Archaeological Society Journal*, 16, 1983, 20–7.

**Chapter 7** (pages 132–46)

1. F.M.L. Thompson, *English Landed Society in the Nineteenth Century*, Routledge & Kegan Paul, 1963, 210.

2. *Ibid.*, 208–9.

3. D. Hey, *Yorkshire from AD 1000*, Longman, 1986, 288.

4. L. Munby, *The Hertfordshire Landscape*, Hodder & Stoughton, 1977, 161.

5. J.H. Bettey, *Church and Parish*, Batsford, 1987, 126–30.

6. M. Batey, 'Nuneham Courtenay: an Oxfordshire 18th Century Deserted Village', *Oxoniensia*, XXXIII, 1968, 108–24; B.A. Box, *The English Parsonage*, John Murray, 1960; B. Jones, *Follies and Grottoes*, Constable, 1953.

7. Quoted by D. Spring, 'English Landowners and Nineteenth Century Industrialism' in J.T. Ward and R.G. Wilson (eds), *Land and Industry*, David & Charles, 1971, 38.

8. G. Biddle, *The Railway Surveyors*, Ian Allen, 1990, 83–109; T. Warner 'The Line of Most Resistance', *Country Life*, 4th April 1991; F.M.L. Thompson, *English Landed Society in the Nineteenth Century*, Routledge & Kegan Paul, 1963, 238–68.

9. J. Betjeman 'Great Central Railway' in *High and Low*, John Murray, 1966, 22.

10. Wiltshire Record Office, Pembroke MSS, 2057/A5/37.

11. This whole subject is discussed by A. Tinniswood, *A History of Country House Visiting*, National Trust, 1989.

12. Dorset Record Office, Weld MSS, D/WLC/E94.

13. *Victoria County History*, Wiltshire XIII, 1987, 82–3.

14. M. Girouard, *The Victorian Country House*, Oxford University Press, 1971, 2.

15. H.A. Clemenson, *English Country Houses and Landed Estates*, Croom Helm. 1982, 143, 152–3, 232–3; J.V. Beckett, *The East Midlands from AD 1000*, Longman, 1988, 322–3; A. Sproule, *Lost Houses of Britain*, David & Charles, 1982.

16. J. Skinner, *Journals*, British Library, Add. MSS. 33,642.

17. Somerset Record Office, Popham MSS, DD/PO.; R. Strong, M. Binney and J. Harris, *The Destruction of the Country House*, Thames & Hudson, 1974.

# Index